Psych ER

Psych ER

Psychiatric Patients Come to the
Emergency Room

René J. Muller

THE ANALYTIC PRESS

2003   Hillsdale, NJ   London

Published by
The Analytic Press, Inc., Publishers
101 West Street, Hillsdale, NJ 07642
www.analyticpress.com

Set in Garamond & Arial by
Christopher Jaworski, Bloomfield, NJ
qualitext@verizon.net

The stories from chapters 1, 3, 4, 9, 11–15, 17, and 19–26 first appeared in *Psychiatric Times*.

Library of Congress Cataloging-in-Publication Data

Muller, René J.
Psych ER : psychiatric patients come to the emergency room /
    René J. Muller
p. cm.
Includes bibliographical references.

ISBN 0–88163–403–4
1. Psychiatric hospitals—Emergency service.
2. Crisis intervention (Mental health services).
3. Mentally ill—Biography.
4. Mental illness—Diagnosis.
5. Pathography.
I. Title.

RC480.6.M84   2003
362.2'04251—dc22
2003062801

Printed in the United States of America
10 9 8 7 6 5 4 3 2

Dedication

To the 30-some ER patients whose stories make up this text, and to the other 2000 or so patients whose stories were heard but are not recorded here—you are the context.

The story . . . is not told by some clever homunculus. Nor is the story really told by *you* as a self because the core *you* is only born as the story is told, *within the story itself.*

When we discover what we are made of and how we are put together, we discover a ceaseless process of building up and tearing down, and we realize that life is at the mercy of that never-ending process. . . . It is astonishing that we have a sense of self at all [achieved partly through telling and retelling the autobiographical story], that we have . . . some continuity of structure and function that constitutes identity, some stable traits of behavior we call a personality.

—A. R. Damasio, *The Feeling of What Happens*

The individual case remains the basic source for all that counts as experience in psychopathology.

—Karl Jaspers, *General Psychopathology*

Psych ER

Preface

Most people come to the emergency room with maladies like high fever, fainting, food poisoning, respiratory crisis, sickle-cell crisis, metabolic imbalance, allergic reaction, infection, seizure, trauma, surgical abdomen, heart attack, and stroke. Others come because what they are feeling, thinking, or doing is understood by them, or by others, to be aberrant.

Many hospitals sponsor a Crisis Intervention Service, a team of mental health clinicians trained to evaluate patients with this kind of—psychiatric—problem. From 1994 to 1999, I worked for the Crisis Intervention Service at Union Memorial Hospital, and since 1999 at Good Samaritan Hospital, both in Baltimore. Although Union Memorial is two blocks from Johns Hopkins University and close to upper-middle-class Guilford and Roland Park, it draws most of its patients from neighborhoods with inner-city populations and inner-city problems. So does Good Samaritan.

Psychiatric patients come to the ER with stories that put them at the center of a crisis in need of resolution. These narratives are condensed by the triage nurse to a few words, which are recorded in the chart as the "chief complaint." The level of distress in these distillates of life experience goes from ordinary unhappiness to despair:

> . . . emotional problems . . . feeling nervous/disturbed by neighbors . . . just wants to talk . . . homeless and cold . . . shaking all over . . . child fighting everyone at home/throwing things around . . . acting abusive and argumentative . . . I feel like I'm going to die . . . depressed/feel like I want to hurt myself and my son . . . I think I need to be hospitalized/no one cares . . . upset and wants a new psychiatrist . . . no sleep for several days . . . stopped taking medication . . . lost medication . . . medication stolen . . . hearing voices . . . seeing things . . . paranoid . . . thinking of suicide . . . I don't want to be here anymore . . . I don't want to live anymore . . . I want to die . . . I want to fucking die . . . I want to die, but I can't . . . If I had a gun I'd shoot myself . . . OD on medication . . . OD on cocaine . . . OD on heroin . . . cut wrists . . . stuck head in oven . . . tried to jump in front of car . . . tried to jump off bridge . . . tried to hang self . . . held knife to throat . . . held gun to head . . . I want to make the police think I have a gun so they will shoot me . . .

These brief phrases in some way capture the reasons patients come to the ER. But people often talk in code, particularly when they are in distress. Part of my job is to sort through the elements of a story and with this information answer the question, What is this patient's life up to? Knowing that, I can determine what needs to be done for the patient in the ER, and what the follow-up should be.

The text ahead comes out of my experience evaluating more than 2000 ER patients over a period of eight years. The 30-some stories selected for telling here add to a large and growing body of medical and psychiatric literature known as pathography—literally, stories about what it means to be ill.

Acknowledgments

I am grateful to Christine Potvin, editorial director of *Psychiatric Times,* to Joy Hought, associate editor, and to the editorial board, for first publishing many of the stories told here; Ronald Pies, M.D. offered tough criticism and kind counsel. I also thank the Reverend David E. Crossley, who made recommendations that helped me to shape and polish this text.

Part I

Straightforward Stories

Each patient I saw in the emergency room was given at least one diagnosis based on the behavioral criteria of the *Diagnostic and Statistical Manual of Mental Disorders*, fourth edition, known colloquially as the *DSM-IV*. Published by the American Psychiatric Association in 1994, this compendium is now the standard followed by mental health clinicians in determining what constitutes a mental disorder. These first 10 stories lead to diagnoses that are often made in the ER.

1　Depression

The World Pushing Down

It is no surprise that a seriously depressed person would head to the ER for help. Many patients who present with depression are already being followed by mental health clinicians and are on antidepressants. Some have stopped their medication; others have recently had negative experiences or new stressors. Many use alcohol and illicit drugs, which can contribute directly (biologically) and indirectly (by interfering with interpersonal relations and work) to depressed mood. Some have lost their ability to function, are suicidal, or have mood-induced psychotic symptoms; these patients are hospitalized. The less seriously depressed patients, after being offered insight and support, are referred back to their providers or for outpatient follow-up with a new provider.

The most common symptoms of major depression are feeling bad most of the day, not enjoying activities that are usually enjoyed, major difficulties with sleeping, eating, or concentrating, thoughts that one might be better off dead, and having a specific plan to end one's life.

Ed gave the distinct impression of being helpless and hopeless. His self-esteem was zero. When I asked if he could imagine what it would take to get beyond his depression, he told me with conviction that he did not know. He didn't seem bothered by his lack of an agenda for getting out of the hole he had dug for himself, or, as he thought of it, the hole his "chemical imbalance" had dug for him. He appeared totally passive with respect to his situation.

I was called to the ER late one evening to evaluate a 50-year-old man who had taken an overdose of his antidepressant medications Remeron and Desyrel. Ed, a diabetic, also claimed to have injected 170 units of short-acting, regular insulin (his daily dose was 15 units).

Ed called his estranged wife and told her what he had done. She immediately phoned a man who lived in the house where her husband rented a room, and he dialed 911.

Ed was lying on a gurney, hooked up to intravenous lines delivering electrolytes and dextrose. His affect was flat: his face had no expression, his voice no modulation. He looked and sounded depressed and described himself as feeling very depressed. "I don't want to live" was his answer when I asked why he had taken the overdose.

The 15 Remeron and 25 Desyrel tablets Ed took were not life-threatening. Without treatment, 170 units of insulin would kill someone with glucose initially in the normal range (60–110 mg/dL). Ed was diagnosed with Type 1 diabetes mellitus 10 years earlier. He had gone off his medication several times, and his glucose typically rose to 400 to 500 mg/dL. Ed told me he was taking the Remeron and Desyrel as prescribed but had stopped the insulin several months earlier. Six hours after Ed reported taking the overdose, he was lethargic but knew who he was, where he was, and the date. He gave adequate, if minimal, answers to all the questions I asked. Ironically, Ed's hyperglycemia, the result of a long furlough from insulin, had saved him. (Ed's glucose level was 136 mg/dL in the ambulance, 90 mg/dL in the ER, and 270 mg/dL after the first infusion of dextrose, given to counteract the insulin overdose.)

Five years earlier, after working there for 20 years, Ed had lost his job as vice-president of operations for a company that made glass products. "I saw it coming," he told me. "They got someone to work cheaper." Ed had a degree in business from a prestigious university. Since being laid off, his life had been what he called a "slow slide downhill." He held several jobs for short periods but hadn't worked for two years. "I've lost everything," he reported without emotion; his loss included the respect of his family. He was living in a rented room, had no money in the bank, and was nearing the end of his unemployment insurance.

Ed's appetite was good, and his weight had stayed constant, but he had not eaten in two days because he couldn't afford to buy food. He was sleeping well. (Normal appetite and sleep are unusual for someone reputedly so depressed.) Ed had been depressed for eight years before losing his job, and saw "many doctors" during that time. Both parents, now deceased, had been diagnosed with depression.

Eight months earlier, intending, he said, to die, Ed had taken an overdose of 100 Tylenol tablets. He did not go for medical treatment. Later, he told his estranged wife about the overdose. She insisted that he sign himself into a psychiatric hospital, where he stayed for 30 days and received electroconvulsive therapy (ECT). Ed was convinced that his depression was due to a "chemical imbalance" and that he could do nothing about it, despite having been told by doctors at the hospital that this was not the case. He insisted that he had not benefited from his contact with any mental health clinician. Remeron and Desyrel had not helped him; neither had ECT. Patients who believe their depression is biologically determined often experience at least a placebo effect with these interventions, but Ed did not.

Ed gave the distinct impression of being helpless and hopeless. His self-esteem was zero. When I asked if he could imagine what it would take to get beyond his depression, he told me with conviction that he did not know. He didn't seem bothered by his lack of an agenda for getting out of the hole he had dug for himself, or, as he thought of it, the hole his "chemical imbalance" had dug for him. He appeared totally passive with respect to his situation. "I'm not ready to get another job," he assured me.

Ed denied having delusions or hallucinations, the distortions of perception that those with severe depression sometimes experience. He had never been paranoid. His *DSM-IV* diagnosis was depressive disorder, recurrent, severe, without psychotic features. Fifteen years earlier, Ed had used cocaine for one year, but not since, and he had not tried any other street drugs. He never abused alcohol.

By phone, Ed's estranged wife confirmed the main points of his story, along with my suspicion that Ed had done little to help himself since losing his job. She had encouraged him to apply for Social Security disability for his depression, an indication that both considered his condition permanent. Ed readily agreed to a voluntary admission to a psychiatric hospital, his second in eight months. Before leaving the ER, I challenged his belief that a "chemical imbalance" made any effort to overcome his depression futile. He stuck to his guns and again insisted he could do nothing to help himself.

How can we understand Ed's situation? This explanation, which fits most of the depressed patients I have seen, comes from the philosopher Jean-Paul Sartre, who is also recognized for his contributions to existential psychoanalysis. Sartre believed that people who become depressed after a negative experience (a loss, defeat, or rejection) trick themselves into believing that they are incapable of going beyond the loss. It is as if one road had closed down and the disappointed person self-indulgently refuses to allow another road to open up. To Sartre, this was an "attitude of excuse" and an act of self-deception.

Through what Sartre called a "magical transformation," the depressed person's formerly instrumental, euthymic world loses its differentiation and, simultaneously, its appeal. The instrumental world is highly differentiated, which is to say a person who lives there values some of its offerings more than others, and selectively responds to its invitations. Differentiating one's world goes hand-in-hand with developing one's self. As the German existential psychiatrist Karl Jaspers explained in his *General Psychopathology*, "increased differentiation brings increased clarity and awareness. Undefined intuitions and feelings give place to clear, definite ideas. From an undifferentiated state of innocence emerge the innumerable contradictions and conflicts of our psychic life." Clearly, differentiation is a prerequisite for psychic health.

An instrumental, differentiated world is a world of cause and effect: projects are started, goals are set, risks are taken. One is willing to be patient, to tolerate setbacks, to overcome obstacles, to defer gratification. In the instrumental world, individuals act as if what they do—how they choose to use the freedom that allows them to construct a world—will influence their fate. Ultimately, depression is a rejection of this kind of world. A depressed person acts as if the requirements for those who live in an instrumental, differentiated, euthymic world no longer apply. As the Dutch psychiatrist J. H. van den Berg put it, the depressed person lives a "different existence."

Clearly, Ed had magically transformed his world by de-differentiating the world he formerly lived in and through. His pathological reconstruction had a flattened terrain, so that what he now saw was uninteresting and unworthy of his attention. His flattened affect (blank facial expression and unmodulated voice) was part of that flatly constructed world. Ed's depression was not *in* him, or in his de-differentiated, flattened, valueless world, but *between* him and that world. It was the *relation* he had to that world. Ed had tricked himself into believing that he could not overcome the disappointment of having lost his job five years earlier (and no doubt other disappointments that came before and after that loss). He had no hope that his life could be different and saw no future for himself. I was surprised that he did not show any signs of anger during our interview. Those feelings, too, may have been ground down and homogenized in the de-differentiation of his world. Ed was in despair.

Ed's choice of a de-differentiated world was made in the context of his "facticity," what Sartre saw as everything a person receives in the throw of the dice that precedes the gift of human freedom: who his parents were, what genes they had passed on, the era he was born into, his social position, his sexual orientation, and so forth. Usually, while evaluating a patient in the ER, I can get a good sense of what these factors are. But Ed had little to say. His answers were strictly factual, short and crisp, with no spontaneous elaboration. He had no insight into his situation and did not seem to want any. Nonetheless, it may be possible to say something about the genetic component of Ed's facticity, since both parents had been treated for depression and he had Type 1 diabetes. Depression is more common in patients whose parents have been depressed, though no one knows what is passed on through the genes here and what is learned at home. Depression is also more common in diabetics, and a direct physiological link between endocrine and mood disorders has been proposed.

Many people lose their jobs and respond instrumentally. Ed may well have been primed by one or more components of his facticity for the passive response he made. His development—how he responded to the challenges presented to him through the life cycle—inevitably figured in as well. There is empirical evidence that, to some degree, life experience is imprinted on the brain's neural substrate, most likely in part through changes in gene expression and the subsequent synthesis of receptor proteins. This imprinting may influence the neural tone of some brain circuits, including those that underlie mood.

I suspect that Ed was rather narcissistic. His body was the shell of a formerly good-looking man. I got the impression that he once was used to having things go his way, and he had a strong sense of entitlement. His de-differentiated world, now tuned solely into himself, may have been tuned there all along. Not once in the interview did he give any indication that his wife or three children had been inconvenienced by the way he was living. During ER evaluations, patients usually express concern about the others they have invariably, if unintentionally, hurt because of their mental illness. Not Ed.

Narcissists overly identify with some ideal scenario of what they feel their lives should be and the role others should play in that scenario. These people take disappointment and loss hard. Their response to negative experience accounts for some of the most virulent pathology associated with this personality trait. I suspect that, after he had lost his job and was being confronted with the shattered image of what he thought his world should be, the structure of Ed's personality predisposed him to de-differentiate that world.

The psychiatrist Viktor Frankl, himself a prisoner of the Nazis during World War II, wrote in *Man's Search for Meaning* about the role choices played in the fate of camp inmates. Some gave up and soon died. Others, constructing for themselves a different kind of world from the fragments of their tragedy, survived, overcoming the injustice that had been done to them. Influenced by Sartre's ideas, Frankl showed that the meaning one gives to negative experience determines how one comes through it. The severity of Ed's depression followed from the number of components of the instrumental world he de-differentiated, and how tightly he held to these transformed constructs. The de-differentiated world he created held him down, leading to his *de-pression*. That world was undoubtedly made of what Hazel Markus calls pathological "self-schemas," patterns of aberrant thinking, feeling, and behavior that cause those who live this way extreme emotional pain and poison their relations with others. In quasi-psychodynamic language, instead of authentically facing, suffering through, and eventually overcoming the pain of his loss by dealing with it in an existential domain, Ed defended against the pain in a psychopathological domain and became depressed.

There are significant points of convergence between Sartre's theory of de-differentiation and the cognitive theory of depression that connects depression to negative thinking. The negative thoughts challenged by cognitive therapists, in what is often a highly effective approach to treating depression, can be seen as the cognitive structural elements of a depressed person's de-differentiated world. These negative thoughts, which are intrinsically pathological and ineluctably lead to depression, need to be distinguished from the negative thoughts that merely make us sad and leave differentiation intact. This kind of cognition is universal, can be part of one's authentic experience, and is compatible with an instrumental construction of the world.

The stress inherent in the lived pathological self-schemas of those who, like Ed, experience major depression almost certainly has a brain correlative. The de-differentiation posited here is simply too radical a deformation of consciousness and too great a consequent stressor to the body *not* to be biologically imprinted. The well-studied hypothalamic–pituitary–adrenal (HPA) axis is a likely major pathway for this imprinting. One can wonder if those persons who de-differentiate their world in this pathological way most strongly and globally are the ones who develop treatment-resistant depression, requiring long courses of high-dose antidepressants or electroconvulsive therapy (ECT). Changes in brain structure and function may act as a "ballast" to perpetuate, through the HPA axis and other routes, the pathological self-schemas that are coincident with de-differentiation.

Just how much of a "brain disease" or "chemical imbalance" Ed had remains a challenging—and for the most part unanswered—question. It is possible that depression's chosen pathological self-schemas are them-selves the essential structural components of depression. The changes seen in brain scans of depressed persons may be secondary phenomena, possibly part of a general stress response. If these changes are not spe-cific to depression, they do not define it. In spite of data accumulated from many empirical studies, the brain–mind gap has not been closed. We do not yet understand how the contents of consciousness are influ-enced by brain structure and function. At present, we do not know enough to say for sure why Ed was depressed.

Panic
The World Coming Apart

Patients suffering panic attacks often come to the ER in terror. Many have physical symptoms, such as heart palpitations, crushing chest pain, and hyperventilation. Some feel they are about to die. Often these patients think they are having a heart attack and are given a chest-pain workup to rule out this possibility.

Some clinicians who specialize in treating anxiety disorders claim that everybody will have at least one panic attack over a lifetime. About 90 percent of those who report panic attacks meet the *DSM-IV*'s criteria for panic disorder. Recurrent, unexpected panic attacks, with persistent concern about having additional attacks and worry about the consequences, along with significant changes in behavior associated with these attacks, are the primary criteria for this disorder.

This sister was the first immediate family member Wendy lost. She had not realized that her sister could die in this way, at that time. At first, Wendy had trouble believing what happened. Then, believing it cost her the sense that she was safe in this world and altered the course of her life.

Wendy was grocery shopping when she suddenly felt a tightness and severe pain in her chest. She could not catch her breath. She felt weak and dizzy. Her arms tingled. Wendy drove herself to the ER.

Once a week during the past year, Wendy, 32, had had a panic attack with these same symptoms. Twenty-five times she went to the ER of three different hospitals. She went by ambulance when the attacks were severe and overwhelming, on her own when they were not. Though Wendy was discharged from the ER each time, she was nevertheless once again convinced she was having a heart attack and that her life was in danger.

For several months, Wendy had been taking Xanax, prescribed by her physician. She had gone once to a community mental health center, but did not return because the psychiatrist there wanted to put her on additional medication. Wendy felt strongly that her problem would not be solved in this way and wanted to be tapered off Xanax. Another psychiatrist she saw cut her dose of the tranquilizer in half.

If the somatic manifestations of Wendy's panic were classic, so was the psychological trauma that almost certainly led to it. A year earlier, her 43-year-old sister died suddenly and unexpectedly in her sleep of a heart attack. The sister had a seizure disorder and lived with her mother because she was not able to take care of herself. Wendy had just left her own house and was in her car, about to drive her younger daughter to her mother's house, when her older daughter rushed out to tell her that their grandmother was on the phone with the news that Wendy's sister had died. Wendy went inside and spoke to her mother. "I dropped the phone," she told me. "I cried and hollered . . . I was devastated . . . I felt this was something unreal . . . I thought they were lying to me."

Wendy then drove to her mother's house. Her other sister and her brother went upstairs to see the dead woman. The woman's arms were raised, and the doctor felt that she had died during a seizure. Not wanting to see the body, Wendy stayed downstairs. "When the undertaker came," she said, "I had to go into the other room." Wendy could not stand to see even her sister's covered body pass through the house. "I was still thinking it wasn't true," she explained. "Why did it have to happen to her?"

This sister was the first immediate family member Wendy lost. She had not realized that her sister could die in this way, at that time. At first, Wendy had trouble believing what happened. Then, believing it cost her the sense that she was safe in this world and altered the course of her life. "Everything changed," she said. At the most basic level, what changed for Wendy was that she was now facing the world with a high degree of anxiety. "Every night I feel if I don't pray, I will not wake up . . . When I do wake up in the morning, I have to shake my husband to see if he is alive. Then I check on the children."

For some people who live this anxiously, the body, too, can become anxious with somatic symptoms. When a certain number of these symptoms are severe enough, often enough, a person is said to have panic disorder. Wendy's first panic attack—the "herald attack"—occurred several weeks after her sister died. She was driving home from work with her husband. He had just told her that earlier that day a neighbor died of a heart attack while shopping at a supermarket. Most likely, hearing about this second sudden death was the "two-punch," the final assault on Wendy's already severely compromised sense of the world as a safe place. That she learned of both deaths while in a car may have increased the emotional trauma of the second death.

During the first panic attack, Wendy felt crushing chest pain, became short of breath, and thought she was dying. Her husband drove her to the nearest ER. A chest-pain workup ruled out a myocardial infarction. The diagnosis was panic attack, and she was discharged with instructions to follow up with outpatient treatment.

Wendy assured me she had never experienced any major anxiety before her sister died. She described herself as having been a happy, sociable person, who enjoyed walking, bike riding, and going out with her husband. "Now," she said, "I'm too afraid to do anything . . . too afraid of having another panic attack . . . I fear going to sleep. That I won't wake up the next morning." Wendy was still able to work as an aide in a nursing home and keep her house in order, but otherwise her life had been severely limited by recurring panic attacks and the fear of the next attack.

"I've been depressed for a year," Wendy told me. Her sleep was reduced to five or six hours a night and was fitful. Her appetite, however, was unchanged and she had not lost weight. Wendy did not have the energy she had formerly, either at home or at work. Family members and coworkers at the nursing home where she worked told her she looked "down." "I have half the interest in sex I used to have," she reported with regret. Wendy's facial expression was frozen in sadness. She walked slowly and tentatively. Her voice was a leaden monotone.

Though Wendy met the *DSM-IV* criteria for major depression, her most disabling symptoms were rooted in anxiety. Clearly, she had all the symptoms required to diagnose panic disorder (many people have both depression and anxiety, and, for some, the anxiety is expressed somatically as panic). Wendy had numerous discrete panic attacks—one a week during the year before I saw her; she worried about having additional attacks; she worried about losing control and having a heart attack; her behavior had been restricted considerably, but not to the point of her being housebound. Though she did have some symptoms of agoraphobia, she was not impaired to the degree that would justify this diagnosis.

Wendy's diagnosis was panic disorder without agoraphobia. She was referred for outpatient treatment. Different interventions have been successful in treating this mental disorder, particularly cognitive, psychodynamic, and behavioral therapies. Cognitive therapy challenges a patient's thoughts and feelings that the world is unfamiliar and unsafe. Psychodynamic therapy addresses the content of feelings underlying the conflict that precedes the "herald attack." Behavioral therapy, exposing a patient directly to the situations that induce panic attacks, reduces the patient's sensitivity to these situations.

Historically, benzodiazepines and tricyclic antidepressants were the first drugs used to oppose the symptoms of panic disorder. Recently, the selective serotonin reuptake inhibitors (SSRIs), particularly Paxil, have become the preferred way to medicate these symptoms. Wendy was taking Xanax. But she knew—and clinical research strongly backs her intuitive understanding—that this drug would not be the ultimate solution: panic symptoms return when medication is stopped. To rid herself of panic attacks, Wendy would have to regain the sense she lost, when her sister died so suddenly and unexpectedly, that the world was at least a minimally safe place—not as unpredictable and unsafe as her traumatic experience had led her to believe.

3   Borderline Personality
A Brittle World, a Labile Mood

Borderline personality disorder is a psychiatric diagnosis given to some patients with a "brittle" self, who have severe, chronic problems dealing with others. These patients often act impulsively and destructively. *Borderline* is a misleading term, implying (wrongly) the tendency of a patient to cross some border into an even more ominous condition, such as psychosis or schizophrenia.

Borderline patients do not do well in close relationships; intimacy is experienced as a further threat to an already shaky self. They do not do well alone either, because not having anyone close to them heightens a chronic, ongoing sense of emptiness. It is as if being close to someone is being too close, and being less close is being too far. Borderline patients cannot establish a satisfying emotional distance in relationships with others—in love, friendship, or work. People with borderline personality disorder have great difficulty getting over rejection or loss of any kind. A negative experience may quickly trigger a depression. Borderline patients often come to the ER after being repudiated in some way. They are angry, depressed, and unable to accept and work through what has happened to them.

As the interview progressed, Heidi's borderline dynamics became more pronounced under the stress of having to tell her story. The ambivalence—that is, her alternating between opposite ways of thinking and feeling about the same person or issue—was particularly striking. Her mother later told me, "With Heidi, everything is either black or white."

Heidi, 31, was brought to the ER by her mother early on a Saturday evening. "Heidi is depressed and suicidal," the mother told me as I walked into the room to begin the interview. The triage note quoted the patient as saying, "I'm not going to do anything, but if I were to get hit by a truck that would be all right." Heidi made it clear that she had no definite plan to hurt herself but added, "I'm not sure about tomorrow." Further questioning revealed that the uncertainty was not over taking her life, but about how she would get through the day.

Heidi was short and slight, with short, curly, brown hair that looked as if it had been sculpted from underneath; the top was full and the bottom cut away. She appeared frightened as she sat, fully clothed, on the gurney, legs in dark, tight-fitting pants, hanging over the side. She quickly acknowledged that the emotion she was most conscious of was anxiety. She looked and sounded scared and defiant. One moment, she seemed eager to tell her story and take me into her confidence. The next, she seemed annoyed that the interview was taking place at all.

Heidi came from an upper-middle-class family and attended private school, but graduated from a high school that emphasized the arts. She spent several years at a prestigious school of design in New York City, but had to drop out, she said, when her father refused to pay her tuition. She held several jobs in the design field and claimed to have successfully completed some significant projects.

A relationship with a lesbian lover (who the mother later told me was abusive) had ended the day before. It was not clear who had initiated the breakup. Heidi had had a difficult year, with several significant setbacks, including the ending of another lesbian relationship while she lived in California, the loss of a house she was buying there, and the loss of her car. She had not had a job in two years. She left California because she was out of money. She was now living with her mother in an apartment in one of the city's better neighborhoods.

Her mother had imposed a 1 a.m. curfew, which Heidi saw as an outrageous restriction for a 31-year-old woman. Later, the mother told me she felt that her daughter needed to be taken care of. It was one of Heidi's many dilemmas that she required her mother's help but strongly resented this dependence. During the interview, she talked alternately like a needy child and like a wildly independent adult. She had no way of reconciling this ambivalence and gave no indication of even feeling that it should be resolved. She seemed resigned to the desperate fate of being caught on the horns of this dilemma. She wore the attitude, What am I supposed to do?

Heidi acknowledged feeling increasingly desperate recently and told me that it seemed as if she were "falling apart." It was hard for her to get through the day and deal with other people. But nevertheless she had some friends. Asked where she got the marijuana, heroin, and cocaine that showed up in her toxicology screen, she said it was from these friends. Heidi had been a binge user of heroin for the last eight years, and of cocaine for the last 13 years. She took these drugs by nose, never intravenously, and went for long periods without using drugs at all.

Heidi had started using marijuana three years earlier. Her parents, who came of age during the 1960s, smoked this drug heavily throughout her childhood, and she hated the smell. It took time, she said, to overcome this aversion. Heidi acknowledged that marijuana dulled the edge of her anxiety, and that she used heroin and cocaine in part to control her labile mood. She had been in a private drug treatment center six years ago but checked herself out after several days.

Heidi's psychiatrist was currently prescribing Ativan and phentermine, an amphetamine sometimes used as an adjunct mood-brightening medication for depression. She had been on a number of antidepressants, but none had worked well for any length of time. Heidi remarked several times during the interview that her medication "wasn't working anymore." She told me this with a tone of disappointment and exasperation that made me think she was holding the medication responsible for this failure, as well as the psychiatrist who prescribed it.

Until recently, Heidi had been seeing a therapist, who she claimed helped her. But the woman had been injured in a car accident and was not seeing patients now. Heidi had had psychiatric treatment on and off since the age of seven, and had been tried on a number of medications, including lithium, with only partial and temporary results. She had never been hospitalized for a psychiatric illness.

Borderline patients—and it fast became clear during the interview that Heidi was showing many features of borderline personality disorder—take loss particularly hard. Their already fragile sense of self and identity is severely challenged by any negative experience. The breakup with her partner the day before probably triggered an exacerbation of anxiety, anger, and depression, as well as the thoughts of being better off dead, that brought her to the ER.

As the interview progressed, Heidi's borderline dynamics became more pronounced under the stress of having to tell her story. The ambivalence—that is, her alternating between opposite ways of thinking and feeling about a person or issue—was particularly striking. Her mother later told me, "With Heidi, everything is either black or white." However, unlike many borderline patients who present to the ER, Heidi did not outwardly lose control or attempt to draw other members of the ER staff into the conflict she was experiencing.

Many (but not all) borderline patients are unable to tolerate or accept ambiguity in their lives—that they, others, and just about everything the world has to offer are to some degree both good *and* bad, positive *and* negative. How can one be sure of how to relate to someone, or to assess a situation, under these conditions? This inability to accept ambiguity derives from an anxiety-driven primitive defense known in the psychoanalytic literature as *splitting*. Splitting is a pathological (and ultimately failed) attempt to keep separate in one's consciousness and behavior the components of ambiguity that make life feel unusually risky so that the ambiguity can be lived in a less anxious way.

No one can ever fully know what to expect from others. Implicitly, most people accept this fact of life. Certain borderline patients, however, are unable to face the anxiety inherent in ambiguity. To avoid the anxiety they cannot tolerate, they view others and the situations they find themselves in alternately as "all good" (while something is seen and felt as fully positive it can be embraced wholeheartedly, without the fear of being hurt), then as "all bad" (the totally negative can be rejected with full certainty). By alternately seeing the situation first from one (unrealistic) view, then the other, the full thrust of the existential anxiety inherent in the unsplit view (achieved by realistically integrating the polar opposite components of ambiguity) is temporarily skirted.

But the price paid for this distortion of reality is high. No one in his or her right mind can tolerate being related to by a borderline patient in this way for any length of time. Imagine being put on a pedestal one moment, only to be dethroned the next, without deserving the extreme either of high praise or condemnation, and without doing anything to deserve the *switch* from one extreme to the other. Imagine how confused and betrayed you would feel if someone related to you in this way for any time.

Obviously, it is difficult to maintain a relationship with such a person, which is one reason why borderline patients have so much trouble with others and why their lives become so chaotic. Clearly, it is impossible to maintain a commitment to another person, or to some project, if the meaning of the experience involved changes radically and often. Borderline patients put themselves outside the loop of consensually shared human experience when they live with this kind of ambivalence. F. Scott Fitzgerald felt that "the test of a first-rate intelligence is the ability to hold two opposed ideas in the mind at the same time, and still retain the ability to function." He might have added that one characteristic of a stable psyche is the capacity to tolerate the opposed emotions associated with these opposed ideas.

Borderline patients who use the splitting defense have even greater difficulty finding a comfortable emotional distance between themselves and others, or a comfortable place within any situation, than borderline patients who do not use it. This, in part, accounts for the high level of anxiety many borderline patients, including Heidi, feel. To be anxious is, ultimately, not to know and sense one's place in the world. Borderline patients act in such a way as to put themselves either too close to, or too far from, the other person or situation, depending on whether they are splitting positively or negatively. If they choose to commit themselves, they commit too much and expect too much from the commitment (to the positive "all-good" view). When they rescind the commitment after their unrealistic expectations are not met, or, if they are unilaterally rejected, they cannot work through the loss and feel abandoned (in the now "all-bad" view). No wonder borderline patients have such excruciating difficulties with love and work—what Freud thought life was all about.

It is no surprise that a borderline patient's sense of self and identity becomes lacerated in this defensive process, causing a heightened vulnerability to loss and to negative experience of any kind. It is impossible to mourn successfully and get over the loss of anyone, or anything, until the true meaning of what has been lost is fully acknowledged. Many borderline patients cannot do this, as they continue to alternate between extreme opposite thoughts and feelings about someone who has died or ended a relationship. One cannot work through a loss while the meaning of the loss constantly changes.

Many people with borderline pathology seek treatment for the first time soon after a significant other has exited their life, as defenses weaken and they experience an increase in borderline symptoms. Heidi came to the ER that Saturday evening, suitcase packed, the decision made—to the extent that any borderline patient can be said to make a decision—to sign herself into the inpatient psychiatric unit one day after the breakup of a serious relationship.

"Black and white" was how Heidi's mother had described her daughter's take on the world. More specifically, Heidi *alternated* between black and white, splitting her thinking and feeling about herself, others, and everything else in her life. During the course of our one-hour interview, and a subsequent two-hour discussion of the question with her mother and me, Heidi decided (many times), then rescinded the decision (many times), to be admitted as an inpatient to the psychiatry unit. During this period, while she was trying to decide what to do, she poured out her heart about how bright and talented she was, how hard she had worked to make something of her life, how many obstacles she had overcome, how many good starts there had been on various projects, how successful some projects had been, how she was praised lavishly for one of them and how she had been offered other jobs. But now she had no job, and no money, and was living with her mother, subject to a curfew.

How had this happened to her? Really, Heidi did not have a clue. Her parents were divorced. The father had remarried, but the mother was still single. Both had been strongly influenced by the counterculture of the 1960s. Now in his mid-50s, the father was a successful industrial designer. He was also an alcoholic, according to Heidi, had used marijuana and stronger drugs, and was highly narcissistic. Her mother had been depressed much of her life and was suicidally depressed for a period of time when Heidi was a teenager. During that time, mother and daughter in effect changed roles, and Heidi nursed her mother through her illness (the mother verified this fact). We can only guess what being caught in that role reversal cost Heidi, who missed no chance to point out how dysfunctional her family was, and how she had been traumatized by the family dynamic. With venomous sarcasm, she told me that her sister, who was considered by her parents to be the good and successful daughter, had a master's degree and was doing well.

After Heidi signed the form for voluntary admission to the inpatient unit, I contacted the on-call psychiatrist. I gave him a detailed summary of my evaluation, along with a recommendation that she be admitted. Though not an imminent danger to herself or anyone else, Heidi, after experiencing several significant losses during the last year, had just lost another significant person in her life, was in a seriously conflicted situation with her mother at home, showed strong signs of decompensation, and seemed in need of what D. W. Winnicott called a "holding environment."

This psychiatrist was new to the department and had his first on-call shift that day. Any of the other staff psychiatrists would have accepted this patient immediately. But, perhaps unsure of his role as inpatient attending psychiatrist, he insisted on coming to the ER—a half hour's drive from his home, in the rain—to do his own interview.

And interview he did, for at least another hour. He spoke with Heidi alone, with the mother alone, and with mother and daughter together. I talked to the mother in the hallway, and she told me the psychiatrist favored hospitalization. She did, as well. But when the psychiatrist finished his interview and came back to my office, he told me that the patient had now decided *not* to be admitted, but to go home with her mother instead.

The psychiatrist (who had done nothing wrong clinically, but seemed embarrassed at the consequences of his intervention), hoping to change Heidi's mind, suggested that all four of us meet one last time. Heidi sat, glum and angry, on a couch in a small room. In his long interview, the psychiatrist had gone over the pros and cons of being treated as an out-patient or inpatient, as I had earlier. Though he made it clear he favored hospitalization, his simply mentioning the possibility of not being admitted after Heidi had signed the form for voluntary admission with my encouragement was probably enough to signal to her that she was about to be abandoned, a totally unrealistic assessment of the offer being made.

Angry and disgusted with me, the psychiatrist, and the situation she found herself in, Heidi said, "You are confusing me. It took me 30 years to get here [to the point of signing herself into a psychiatric hospital], and now . . ." And now, unable to handle what she saw as a newly introduced and frightening ambiguity, she would drop us before we could (in her mind) drop her. "Home is starting to look pretty good," she said with conviction. Two hours earlier, with equal conviction, she had told me that home was "unbearable."

Suitcase in hand, and feeling once again that the world had treated her badly, Heidi went home with her mother. How many times, through how many situations, and with how many people had Heidi made this same kind of defensive choice? And how many times would she repeat this defensive behavior, and with what terrible consequences? Like many borderline patients, Heidi luxuriated in her anger (perhaps the most perversely gratifying of all the negative emotions), blamed her problems on everyone else, and expected any change for the better to come from the outside, not from her own efforts.

This said, it should be acknowledged that Heidi, by declining to be hospitalized, may, ironically, have not made a bad choice after all. Borderline patients have a tendency to regress in psychiatric units, partly because their needs to be passive and taken care of are fed. The muted hospital environment benefits patients like Heidi mainly when they are so anxious or depressed that they cannot take care of themselves, or when they become a direct threat to themselves or others. Initially, I felt Heidi met the first criterion. In retrospect, it seems that, confronted with the choice between what she saw as the ambiguous circumstances of a possible inpatient admission and the ambiguities of her situation outside the hospital, she took the latter to be less threatening.

4   Multiple Personality

Taking on the World with More Than One Identity

Multiple personality disorder is the old name for what the *DSM-IV* now calls dissociative identity disorder (DID). *Dr. Jekyll and Mr. Hyde,* from the 19th century, and *The Three Faces of Eve,* from the 20th, are stories that have etched the bizarre nature of this mental illness into popular consciousness.

Though the validity of the DID diagnosis is questioned by a number of mental health clinicians, for at least some patients this purported scission of feeling, thinking, and behavior into more than one viable personality seems to be a real phenomenon. Dr. Jekyll, Mr. Hyde, and Eve probably represent the extreme of personality dissociation and are examples of how strongly this phenomenon may be lived out by one person. The question of how much a DID patient contributes to creating alternate personalities has yet to be answered.

A 10-inch piece of rubber tourniquet hose, a bent straw, and a tampon that Nadine said had been soaked in bleach were removed. She later told me that the hostile alter who put these objects into her vagina was also trying to "poison" her by mouth. "Up here I have control," she said, pointing to her mouth. "Down here," indicating the genital area, she implied that her control was tenuous.

D issociative identity disorder (DID), known as multiple personality disorder until renamed by the *DSM-IV* in 1994, is a controversial diagnosis. Many highly regarded clinicians have built careers working with patients they believe to have DID. Other distinguished practitioners consider DID a bogus diagnostic tag.

Paul R. McHugh, Professor of Psychiatry at Johns Hopkins, argues vigorously that hysteria—what he sees as the DID patient's "more or less unconscious effort to appear more significant to others and to be more entitled to their interest and support"—along with the current social canonization of the victim account for the fanciful behavior of those who claim to have multiple identities and personalities. H. Merskey, Professor of Psychiatry at the University of Western Ontario, believes that the rise in DID diagnosis can be traced to the 1957 book *The Three Faces of Eve,* later made into a film, and to other books and films about DID, and to the uncritical affirmation of the diagnosis by a large number of mental health clinicians. Merskey claims his research failed to identify a single "uncontaminated" DID case originating in a defensive response to trauma, the psychodynamic mechanism thought to underlie DID.

McHugh, Merskey, and other critics of DID all essentially agree that the behavior named by this diagnosis is socially learned. Highlighting the interaction of patient and culture, Merskey sees the behavioral productions associated with DID as the "manufacture of madness." McHugh calls the diagnosis a "psychiatric misadventure." (The *DSM-IV* bases diagnosis solely on behavior, leaving the meaning of the behavior unspecified.)

Perhaps some patients—but probably not most given the DID diagnosis—experience a trauma-induced, psychodynamically based dissociation and fragmentation of feeling, thinking, and behavior sufficient to allow coalescence around two or more distinct identities. Whatever the origin of their dissociated behavior, those who meet criteria for DID have frequent exacerbations of their symptoms and often come to the ER in crisis.

Nadine, 23, acted in a way consistent with the supposition of dissociated identities to a greater degree than any other patient I have worked with (how she came to act this way and what her actions meant are ultimately unknown). This was the third time I had been asked to see Nadine in the ER. She was sitting on a royal blue mattress in the seclusion room, watched and comforted by a female technician who had a particularly gentle way with patients.

Nadine seemed to be holding court, alternately speaking English and Russian, a language she later told me she had studied seriously. Her speech was rapid and pressured, loud and emphatic. Much of what she said was intelligible, some was not. She wrote in a notebook as she spoke, making bold strokes that produced lines and, occasionally, a few words. Nadine was childlike in appearance and manner, short, and slightly built, with short brown hair and thick glasses that seemed too big for her sharp-featured, feral face.

Nadine had come from the oncology unit upstairs. Proudly, she flashed a hospital badge with her picture and *VOLUNTEER* printed in bold, black letters. She gave two reasons for coming to the ER. First, she needed prescriptions for Paxil, Desyrel, and Synthroid, because her psychiatrist was on vacation and was not due back for two weeks. The second reason was that, as she put it, "the children started coming out." These "children," as far as I could tell, were several of the more immature facets of her identity—the "alters"—who tended to cause trouble for the major identity, "Nadine" (a name she chose, not her legal first name).

Whoever was speaking for the ensemble of labile identities constituting the consciousness of this patient (ostensibly Nadine) gave an agreeable and often cogent interview. Much of what she said made sense, but some did not and was clearly bizarre. Both the cogent and the bizarre were put forward with equal conviction, making me think that she could not distinguish one from the other.

Nadine was hyperalert and knew who she was (i.e., "Nadine"), the name of the hospital, and the date. Her speech was rapid, had a stop-and-start quality, and was loud and poorly modulated. Asked about her mood, she said she felt "sad" but denied any disturbance of sleep or appetite; weight loss; anhedonia; psychomotor retardation (she had been agitated earlier, most likely because of anxiety, but was relatively calm during the interview); extended disturbance of daily routine (she had come to us directly from her volunteer work); or thoughts of being better off dead. She denied any intent or plan to hurt herself or anyone else. She insisted that her father had abused her physically and sexually.

Four months earlier, Nadine had been discharged from a state mental institution following a one-year stay. She lived in a group home for two months after that but was asked to leave when the staff could no longer provide the attention she needed "to control the children," the immature alters who caused Nadine to lose control. Currently, she was living with a female friend.

Nadine told me she wanted to get the prescriptions for her medication and go home. She assured me she could now manage on her own. She denied any history of alcohol or substance abuse (the toxicology screen was negative). Her physical health was currently good, she said, though she did have asthma and was taking Synthroid for hypothyroidism.

Almost parenthetically, Nadine let it be known that while she was in a bathroom a few feet from the seclusion room "a man shoved garbage up me." I did not take her claim literally, though I repeated the remark to a physician assistant, who immediately said no to her own unspoken thought of doing a pelvic examination.

When I finished the interview, I spoke with the ER attending, who agreed to give Nadine the prescriptions she asked for and discharge her. We were busy that evening, and Nadine had to wait for her chart to be signed and for me to write follow-up orders for her discharge. Sitting on one of the high stools that ring the nurses' station, she took her place among several of the ER staff and talked confidently with them.

When I brought the discharge form for her signature, Nadine repeated what she had said during the interview about garbage being inserted into her while she was in the bathroom. When I did not respond, she quickly become agitated and refused to sign the form. "You promised to help me with this," she said, not saying who made the promise. Later, she insinuated that it was the female technician who had watched her in the seclusion room.

Agitation quickly gave way to hysterics. The patient (whatever facet of her dissociated, fractured identity was paramount now, possibly not Nadine) was screaming, and drawing the attention of the ER staff and other patients. In a few seconds, she went from what appeared to be a composed young woman (Nadine?) to a hysterical child (an alter?), screaming that we were not giving her the attention we had promised.

Followed by a male technician, Nadine left the ER area and wandered past the radiology waiting room, down a hall leading to the south wing of the hospital. She was clearly out of control now but eventually took our suggestion to go back to the waiting room. She refused several chairs in the empty room and chose instead to sit in a corner, legs pulled up, head down. After about 15 minutes, she was calm enough for us to coax her back to the seclusion room.

Having seen part of this display, the ER attending insisted that Nadine be admitted to the hospital's psychiatric unit. Loudly objecting, Nadine became agitated again and demanded to be discharged. I suggested we wait to see if she would regain her composure, and then reevaluate. But the consensus among the ER staff was for admission, and I did not disagree strongly enough to pursue the point.

Nadine called her therapist from a phone at the nurses' station and spoke intently for some time. I went back to the office to work on my report, which had to be finished before she could go upstairs to the psychiatric unit. Then I got a call from Nadine's therapist, who told me that as far as she was concerned Nadine had been "certifiable" all week; that Nadine sometimes did insert objects into her vagina; and that she would fight being hospitalized "tooth and nail."

On the chance that the patient (whoever she was now, either Nadine or one of "the children") might have become more rational in the half hour it took me to finish writing the report, and hoping to save the extra time and labor involved in the certification, I asked her to sign herself in voluntarily. Seated just a few feet down the hall from the office, she was talking to a young male patient who was sitting on a gurney, legs over the side. In the few seconds I had to survey the situation, it seemed they were communicating rationally and happily. Anticipating my request, she said before I could get a word out, "I will sign a voluntary. I just need a day or two in the hospital. I don't want to cause any trouble." Nadine was back, or so it seemed.

Two days later, I called the attending psychiatrist who had accepted Nadine for the inpatient unit. Gynecology had been asked for a consult, did a pelvic examination, and removed from her vagina a quantity of debris that could have come from an ER bathroom wastebasket.

During an ER visit several months earlier, while waiting to be seen, Nadine had specifically asked for a female attending to take out objects that, she said, had been placed in her vagina by a hostile alter. A 10-inch piece of rubber tourniquet hose, a bent straw, and a tampon that Nadine said had been soaked in bleach were removed. She later told me that the hostile alter who had put these objects into her vagina was also trying to "poison" her by mouth. "Up here I have control," she said, pointing to her mouth. "Down here," indicating the genital area, she implied that her control was tenuous.

Nadine's claim that "a man shoved garbage up me" first struck us as a delusion. Considering the alleged history of physical and sexual abuse by her father, and following the DID dynamic model, one could ask whether a hostile alter (a "part" of her consciousness not under her control) may have reenacted her father's original violation. In her panoply of dissociated identities, where the trauma with the father was not integrated into the structure of one personality, could one alter have taken up the role of the intrusively violating parent? Or, alternatively, could Nadine, deceiving herself, have done what her culture and the mental health clinicians she worked with told her a hostile alter of someone with DID would be expected to do?

Many mental health clinicians who believe in the DID diagnosis insist that the main personality (for this patient, Nadine) is a borderline personality. Taken as one person and one identity, Nadine does come off as thoroughly borderline. Indeed, some who do not acknowledge the validity of the DID diagnosis claim that DID patients are really just severe borderlines. But, clearly, even borderline patients who are very labile do not have emotions and behaviors that coalesce around strikingly different identities to the extent that many patients diagnosed with DID, including Nadine, do. If someone with DID can ultimately be considered borderline, he or she must be seen as a very different kind of borderline, perhaps one with hysterical features severe enough also to warrant the diagnosis of histrionic personality disorder.

Sometimes, while we are trying to distinguish one mental disorder from another, a point is reached when thinking diagnostically seems futile. This may be the time to quit trying to fit a patient's symptoms to one set of diagnostic criteria or another, so that the fundamental question of why a patient's life is being lived as it is can be asked more directly and concretely. If one believes that multiple personalities are purposefully created by the patients themselves, then the task would be to discover why Nadine felt it necessary to distribute her Being over so many fragmented beings, and why the usual degree of personality integrity did not work for her.

5   Alcohol

Chemically Altering
One's World by Mouth

When those who abuse alcohol and drugs come to the ER, we see them in the desperate situations their addiction has put them in. Often coping with the misery and degradation of withdrawal, which comes only hours after the last use of the substance or substances they abuse, these patients seem far from the "heightened" state they so recently enjoyed. Unwilling to do the work of authentically feeling well, substance abusers inauthentically alter their world by directly changing their brain chemistry—in effect, bypassing the efforts that those who live in the instrumental world of cause and effect must make to achieve their more tempered states of satisfaction. This chemically induced self-deception is what mental health clinicians point to when they insist that substance abusers are really "self-medicating" their anxious and depressed feelings.

It is not difficult to understand why someone with this kind of family situation, who drank as much alcohol as Kate did, would be depressed. Few of Kate's basic needs were being met. Drinking made dealing with her issues and conflicts all but impossible. Every day, she chemically altered her experience so it temporarily felt less unpleasant and threatening. But every day, even while she denied it, the situation she was trying to avoid became even more unpleasant and threatening.

In a period of just over three years, Kate came to our ER approximately 80 times. Typically, she would call 911 from her home, saying she had been drinking heavily and was suicidal. Her blood alcohol level (BAL) on arrival was usually between 200 and 450. The charts documenting her visits in medical records occupied six inches on a shelf. During one week, we saw her three times.

Kate must have occupied every treatment room at one time or another, waiting for her BAL to fall to 80 or less, so she could be interviewed. During most visits, she eventually withdrew her threat of suicide and agreed to return home. When things were particularly bad for her and she could not face going home, she stuck to her threat of self-harm and was admitted to the inpatient psychiatric unit.

Kate, 46, had been drinking up to a fifth of vodka a day for 15 years. During that time, she had periods of sobriety lasting from a few months to many months. She had been to several outpatient detox programs but followed up only for short periods, if at all. She refused inpatient treatment. She joined Alcoholics Anonymous, went to meetings, and had several sponsors. While professing great admiration for this program, she invariably drifted away. Kate denied ever using street drugs. She did not smoke cigarettes. Her father had also been dependent on alcohol.

For a time, Kate was followed at a community mental health center. Later, she enrolled in a partial hospitalization program. She was compliant to a degree but eventually started drinking again and discontinued treatment. She was tried on Antabuse and Revia but eventually drank while on both medications.

Kate's ER presentations had a numbing similarity. When paramedics arrived at her house, she would tell them she was suicidal but stated no specific plan. Her single documented effort to harm herself occurred in 1994 when she took a large overdose of Paxil and Procardia. She was taken to another hospital and admitted to intensive care. Unlike many people who are dependent on alcohol, Kate was usually polite and cooperative while in the ER. She would even apologize for her frequent appearances and say she regretted any inconvenience she might be causing us.

The mother of six children, Kate lived with her 19-year-old daughter and 25-year-old son, who was diagnosed with schizophrenia. This young man did not stay on his medication and frequently became agitated. His disorderly behavior at home contributed to Kate's essentially constant dysphoria. She had been divorced two years earlier and was not on good terms with her ex-husband. The couple had operated a tree removal business together. Kate was now unemployed and had financial problems.

In the ER, Kate would often begin the interview by saying, "I have nothing to live for." It seemed to me that she called 911 because she felt lonely, isolated, and overwhelmed. The ER was a familiar place, where she could be sure that some of her immediate needs would be met. More than once, as she was being given dinner, she told me she did not have the money to eat properly. Somehow, though, she maintained her weight.

Depression was a key feature of Kate's presentations. Her mood was low, her sleep interrupted and not restful, her appetite down. She lacked the energy to maintain her house. She could not cope with her schizophrenic son. Nothing interested her or gave her pleasure. She did not see how she could improve her situation. By the end of the interview, however, she usually withdrew the threat of suicide that had been her ticket to the ER.

It is not difficult to understand why someone with this kind of family situation, who drank as much alcohol as Kate did, would be depressed. Few of Kate's basic needs were being met. Drinking made dealing with her issues and conflicts all but impossible. Every day, she chemically altered her experience so it temporarily felt less unpleasant and threatening. But every day, even while she denied it, the situation she was trying to avoid became even more unpleasant and threatening. Besides keeping her from dealing with the world and others in an instrumental and authentic (not chemically "softened") way, alcohol almost certainly contributed directly (biologically) to her depressed mood. Kate's diagnosis, in addition to alcohol dependence, included alcohol-induced mood disorder.

It is remarkable that after she had been using vodka hard for 15 years, Kate's body did not show more signs of damage. Though she did look older than her 46 years and had hypertension, there was no evidence of cirrhosis or alcoholic hepatitis. Her liver function tests were within normal limits, except for a slightly elevated total bilirubin.

In the ER, Kate never had delirium or grand mal seizures, the severe complications of alcohol withdrawal. On occasion, when she was trembling and sweaty, she was given Librium, Ativan, or Catapres. During various inpatient admissions, Paxil and Prozac were prescribed for depression, and BuSpar for anxiety. None of these medications had much effect. She was also given thiamine and folate to help offset the nutritional deficiency common in those who drink alcohol excessively.

The number of pure alcoholics who come to the ER is relatively small. Many drug abusers and patients with bipolar disorder or schizophrenia have significant problems with alcohol and come in with high blood alcohol levels. If Kate is atypical in this way, she is typical in another way: Until abusers of alcohol or of any other drug stop using that substance, the issues, conflicts, and defenses that make up the "psychological" part of their problem cannot be successfully addressed in therapy. Kate's failure to benefit from outpatient treatment programs or from Alcoholics Anonymous owes much to her continued immersion in alcohol. As time went on, she became less capable of coming to terms with her divorce, her social isolation, and her schizophrenic son. She grew more desperate, drank more, and continued to call 911, all the time increasing the disgust she felt for herself and driving the wedge between herself and others deeper.

Kate went through the familiar mental health "revolving door," chasing her tail. After three years and several months of "revolving" through our ER, she was sent for an extended period to a state hospital, where, as of this writing, she continues to reside.

6   Drugs

Chemically Altering
One's World by Nose and Vein

Writing as long ago as 1858, the French poet Baudelaire called the inauthentic states achieved by those who use drugs "artificial paradises." It is not surprising that the lie inherent in making this transformation should carry over into whatever else the substance abuser does in the instrumental world that is shunned for a chemically induced "paradise." The full impact of this essential lie is often seen when drug addicts come to the ER.

A number of addicts who come to the ER have simply found it too difficult at this point to continue their habit. In essence, they ask us to help them out with a stay in the psychiatric unit for a few days until they can gather the resources needed to go on with their addiction.

"We are educated several levels higher than they are. How do they think they can get away with this?" Showing disbelief and exasperation he had difficulty controlling, an ER attending asked me this question as he was discharging a man in his mid-20s who claimed to be experiencing the latest in a series of episodes of left-flank pain that he insisted could be relieved only by a narcotic analgesic.

An IVP (intravenous pyelogram)—an X-ray of the renal pelvis and ureter, areas where kidney stones form—was negative, a good indication that there was no stone. But a urine sample had shown a trace of blood, a finding consistent with a kidney stone. The attending was suspicious because this patient had come to the ER several times before with the same story. Each time he had a negative IVP and a positive urine test for occult blood. The young man had not followed through with repeated urology clinic referrals, in spite of claiming to be in serious pain.

The attending was now convinced that, whenever this patient gave a urine sample, he pricked his finger with a pin—a drop of blood added to the sample would be enough to give a positive test for occult blood—an old drug-seeker's ER trick, he assured me. The chart from the patient's last visit less than a month before noted that another doctor had given him the narcotic analgesic he asked for. This attending's anger was easy to understand: He had been deceived—but not fooled—by someone who tried to use him to get a controlled substance to feed an addiction.

This clinical tale, with a plot twist, parallels the story told in the ER every day by those dependent on illicit (as contrasted with controlled) substances. Instead of asking for a prescription drug to take away a non-existent symptom, the patient dependent on an illicit substance, or combination of substances, claims to be suicidal and demands a bed in the psychiatric unit.

Why? Because drug addicts (a less generous term for substance-dependent patients) get themselves into trouble in the problematic and often dangerous drug culture that supports their habit. When addicts can no longer negotiate a settlement of their issues within the drug culture, they may try to force themselves into a safer world, where they will be temporarily protected and fed. One refuge is the psychiatric unit. To get a bed—the proverbial "three hots and a cot"—an addict comes to the ER claiming to be suicidal.

Addicts arrive in crisis, but seldom the kind of crisis they claim. They may be broke, homeless, hungry, and dirty. They may have no friends or social support system. Often, a mother or father, sister or brother, significant other, or drug treatment counselor has asked them to leave an apartment, a house, or a treatment program. The most common reasons for these evictions from the hearts and homes of their benefactors (or enablers, as the case may be) include using drugs again after a period of being clean or stealing money or possessions (typically, TVs, VCRs, stereos, and jewelry), disrupting the household, and violent behavior.

Many times, in the middle of the night, I have called a relative or spouse of an addict only to be told—in a tone of voice I have come to recognize as a blend of resignation and despair—that an ER patient I am evaluating has just been told to leave the house for one of those offenses. I ask if the person on the other end of the line would consider taking the patient back if he or she agreed to enter a drug treatment facility. Often, the no comes back with a degree of emphasis one rarely hears. Robert Frost wrote, "Home is that place where, when you have to go there, they have to take you in." But Robert Frost probably did not know any drug addicts.

These fathers and mothers, sisters and brothers, spouses and significant others have been betrayed once too often. They now no longer *care* what happens to the addict in the ER who is threatening suicide. This does not surprise me. What does surprise me are those times when someone on the other end of the line, in the middle of the night, who has been betrayed multiple times by an addict now lying about wanting to end his or her life, is actually willing again to face the prospect of yet another betrayal by this person. This does not happen often.

Addicts frequently come to the ER threatening to hurt themselves because some associate from the drug culture is threatening to hurt them. This threat, unlike that of their own of self-harm, is often genuine. Money not paid in a drug deal, delivery of drugs not up to the standards of the streets, or some other glitch in the commerce of the drug culture is often grounds for serious injury or murder. "I owe someone on the street" is an acknowledgment I have heard many times from addicts whose stories of intended self-destruction I have just punctured.

One heroin addict came to the ER with superficial cuts to both wrists made with a dull razor blade. He claimed to be suicidal because a close friend had recently been shot dead on a street corner. This friend had been a drug dealer, and the patient acknowledged that his death was related to a dispute over a recent drug deal. I called the patient's mother to get her perspective on her son's drug problem and suicide potential. I asked if she knew of this killing. "Many of my son's friends have been killed," she said, with a note of understanding and resignation that broke through the haze of a 6:30 a.m. wake-up call. Clearly, she was unimpressed with the news.

A number of addicts who come to the ER have simply found it too difficult at this point to continue their habit. In essence, they ask us to help them out with a stay in the psychiatric unit for a few days until they can gather the resources needed to go on with their addiction. Some are broke; others are "strung out." Heroin addicts ask for something to "take the edge off" their withdrawal, usually Catapres or Buprenex. Patients dependent on cocaine want something for their depression, which the most honest of them will admit is the downside of the cocaine high. On the street, the demand is strong for tricyclic antidepressants to deal with this kind of mood alteration.

This story of a particularly memorable cocaine and heroin addict illustrates how a malingerer's story, well told and maintained under challenge, can get the malingerer several days of surcease from the hard knocks of drug addiction. "I've had suicidal thoughts for the last three days" was the opening salvo of this 26-year-old man's pitch for a bed. He had been diagnosed with the human immunodeficiency virus (HIV) a year earlier but had not followed up at the clinic where the diagnosis was made. He stated that the "mumbling sounds" he had been hearing in his head for the last three days made him feel suicidal (he could not hear any distinct words in these sounds). "I feel like ending it," he said. How, I asked? "Any way, it doesn't matter," was the reply. Later, he added that if he left the ER he would walk in front of a car on the street outside the ER. This is known as upping the ante: If one threat does not appear to be getting the desired result, make a stronger one.

The patient's affect was essentially flat. Asked what his mood was like, he replied "desperate," which was probably the biggest clue he gave to why he had come to the ER. He reported reduced sleep and appetite. Asked if he felt this was related to his use of crack cocaine, he said he thought it was. I ask all addicts who claim to be suicidal if they have a place to spend the night—in other words, if they are homeless. This patient stated that he had been living with his mother for an extended period, and, in answer to my question, said that yes, he had spent the last two nights at his mother's house. I called the mother to verify this point. She had not seen her son for the last four months. He lived on the streets, she said, and "was out getting high." As far as she knew, he had never made a direct attempt to hurt himself.

With addicts who appear to be angling for a bed in the psychiatric unit, I always check the charts from prior ER visits. As I was leafing through this patient's old records, I spotted a report with my signature dated six months earlier. His story then was similar to the current one, but his suicide threat was less explicit. He had been discharged with a referral to a community mental health center, which, he told me, he did not follow up on. Another record in the chart was from a hospitalization in our psychiatric unit 10 months earlier. The patient had come to the ER claiming to have taken 25 Tylenol tablets, but the toxicology screen did not support this claim.

It may have been the patient's explicit threat to step in front of a car on the street in front of the ER that scared the attending enough so she wouldn't sign her name to a discharge. She and I both tried to talk the patient down from his suicide threat, but he would not budge. He was admitted to the psychiatric unit.

As I was doing the paperwork for the admission, I remembered the words of the ER attending that open this chapter: "We are educated several levels higher than they are. How do they think they can get away with this?" Apparently, by telling a story scary enough to make a doctor think that his or her medical license may die along with the patient's suicide.

With many addicts who threaten suicide if denied a hospital bed, the attending and I openly agree that the chance of the patient actually following through on the threat is nil, particularly when we have hospital records showing that the patient has tried this ploy many times before. But if patients say the right things and do not back off their story when challenged, they may be admitted—even though we realize that, while protecting ourselves, we are also abetting the malingering of people who broke the law by using illicit substances and more than likely broke the law too to get the money to buy them.

Not all those who lie about their intentions to hurt themselves or others are admitted, however. We—an ER attending and I—have called the bluff of many addicts who threatened us. We have sent them out the door to face the consequences of what they had done to themselves. Our implicit message here is: face life on life's terms—precisely what addicts try to avoid doing by using drugs. Of dozens of cases handled in this way, not one has come back to us a reported suicide. We have made an implicit distinction here among those patients who we felt would benefit from inpatient treatment, those who would not but who had somehow outmanipulated us, and those whose lies were so transparent that we felt we did not have to take them at face value.

I have come to recognize the attempts of patients desperate to get a bed to up the ante and say whatever they think will get them admitted. I have found the following question to be a good acid test for the sincerity of a claim of self-harm: "Are you saying that, if you are not admitted, you will harm yourself?" When patients quickly and assertively respond, "Yes, that's it," in a tone suggesting they think they have me on the ropes, I respond by saying, "But that sounds more like a threat than a real commitment to hurt yourself." At this point, the ante may be raised still further. Two of the most memorable ultimate threats from drug addicts I have evaluated are "I know what I have to do" and "I don't want to be here anymore."

Clinicians respond differently to threats at this level, depending on a number of factors, including their own past experience with this kind of patient, how accurately they feel they can read the subtext of a patient's story, and their own level of comfort with the ambiguities such a case presents. Many clinicians prefer to follow the rule: if you are going to err, err on the side of caution. My red flag for patients who claim to be suicidal is a sense they communicate to me of having little or no hope of being able to go beyond the despair they feel in the ER.

This second story of a drug addict represents a somewhat different kind of manipulation. The patient, a 43-year-old man, came to the ER on an emergency petition taken out by the police, who had been contacted after he told his therapist at the community mental health center where he was being followed that he had thoughts of hurting someone else. His opening words to me were, "I want to kill some people, four drug dealers. They sold me some bad dope. It does not get me high."

He had bought $500 worth of this "bad dope," used some for himself, and sold the rest to eight other addicts. He denied it at first, but after repeated questioning he acknowledged that these other addicts were angry at him. He felt that one of them was currently a threat to his life. The patient said he had been thinking of using a gun he kept at home to kill the person who sold him the bogus drugs but decided to go instead to the community mental health center to "explain" himself.

"I need to be in a psycho ward," he told me. "I am a danger to myself and other people." Asked if he had a specific plan to hurt himself and others, he replied that he would "swallow a razor blade" and "shoot the dealer who stiffed me." I regret missing the chance to ask him why he felt the need to swallow a razor blade before getting back at the dealer. He told me that he had been released from prison just over a year earlier, after being convicted of "shooting a junkie in the leg." I called the prison, and they verified that he had done time there for this offense.

The patient acknowledged using cocaine and heroin intravenously ("speedballing") for 15 years, including the period when he was incarcerated. His current use was three dime bags of cocaine and four dime bags of heroin a day. He had used both drugs together the day before. He also used marijuana daily, and LSD occasionally, and currently drank a fifth of Jack Daniel's a day. The toxicology screen was positive for cocaine and heroin, but negative for alcohol.

The patient was given Haldol in prison, he told me, "because I was hearing voices." He had not taken this medication for some time. During the interview, he said that he heard voices when he used drugs. He last heard a voice four hours earlier—his father saying, "Come to hell."

Substance abusers often claim to hear voices. They do this to get a psychiatric diagnosis (usually schizophrenia, schizoaffective disorder, or bipolar disorder), which increases their chance of getting disability compensation and of being admitted to a psychiatric unit when life as a drug addict becomes too difficult. They well know that the mental health profession has greater sympathy for patients diagnosed with these disorders than for those who are just substance abusers.

Asked where he got the money to support a clearly expensive addiction to drugs and alcohol, the patient replied, "I rob and I steal." His last holdup was two days earlier, he told me without embarrassment. He got $40. Did he hurt his victim? I asked. "I slapped his face," he replied. The patient was admitted voluntarily to the psychiatric unit.

My report on this case concludes, "The patient's cooperation and cool demeanor during the interview belie his threats of violence." To this day, I believe that this addict, who threatened to swallow a razor blade (before shooting the dealer who sold him "bad dope"), made up this story to save himself from the wrath of some other addict he had shortchanged, by inadvertently drawing him into this deception. It could be said that, in both this case and in the previous one, admitting the patient amounted to erring—too much—on the side of caution (this case was early in my ER career).

Not all addicts who come to the ER threaten to kill themselves if they are not given a psychiatric bed. Some are genuinely horrified by what their habit has done to them and to others. Of the hundreds of addicts I have interviewed in the ER, one 30-year-old woman stands out from the few I saw as having the desire and the personal resources necessary to seriously confront their addiction.

"I need help. I have started using drugs again." These were Nilda's first words after I asked why she had come to the ER. Her two sisters brought her in after she told them that she had relapsed into an addiction to crack cocaine and heroin. Shortly after Nilda began using these drugs seven years earlier, she had a severe stroke that her doctor felt had been caused by cocaine. She required a long period of rigorous physical and psychological rehabilitation. Nilda had to learn to walk, speak, and perform many of the functions of daily living all over again. She was still using a cane, and her right hand was weak, though her speech showed no trace of impediment.

After discharge from the rehabilitation facility, Nilda went to Narcotics Anonymous and stayed off drugs for about five years. But a year and a half before coming to the ER, in the face of pressures she said she could not handle, she again used crack cocaine and heroin regularly, and marijuana occasionally. Nilda was able to hide this relapse from her family. But under recent mounting pressures, including moving into an apartment and living on her own, Nilda increased her drug use to the point where she felt extremely guilty about betraying her family. They had supported her recovery and were convinced that her addiction was under control.

Nilda had been spending between $10 and $100 on most days for cocaine, which she inhaled (she had not used heroin for six or seven weeks). She was also smoking a marijuana joint every other day. The toxicology screen was positive for cocaine and marijuana.

Nilda's sad appearance matched the description she gave of her inner experience. She spoke slowly and in a low voice that had no modulation. Nothing had seemed good to her for the last two months. During that time, her sleep was down from the usual eight hours to between three and five hours. Nilda was eating less than usual. Thoughts that she would be better off dead (then she wouldn't have these problems) crossed her mind. But she had no current plan to harm herself and had not harmed herself in the past. Guilt was a constant companion. Nilda was depressed in the way that many who use drugs heavily become depressed. This depression derives from both stressful and negative life events and the direct physiological action of addictive substances on the brain.

Convinced that Nilda was willing to take the next step to address her serious addiction a second time, I asked what she felt that step should be. "I'm afraid that if I go home I will use drugs again." I asked her sisters if they would help. One sister, who lived in an apartment with her two children, immediately volunteered to take Nilda in for as long as it took to find a rehabilitation program. Few addicts who come to the ER can go directly to a drug treatment facility, as those diagnosed with a mental disorder can go directly to an inpatient psychiatric facility if its exacerbation is judged to be sufficiently acute. Most insurance plans will not authorize inpatient drug treatment unless patients are felt to be an imminent danger to themselves or others or if they meet the requirements for "medical necessity"—acute withdrawal or a life-threatening medical complication.

Nilda was covered by Medicare because of the residual effects of her stroke. This would give her a better chance of finding a treatment program than many of the addicts who come to the ER without insurance. But with more addicts seeking treatment than facilities available to accommodate them, there was no telling how long it would take her to get into one.

Seeing these three sisters together, I felt the kind of hope for Nilda's eventual recovery that I rarely feel as I fill out the discharge papers for addicts. Most addicts, if the statistics on relapse are accurate, will use drugs again at the earliest opportunity. My hope was rooted in the fact that Nilda had previously held her addiction under control for five years, currently felt considerable guilt about betraying her family, and would now have the support of that family in facing the pressures ahead.

My optimism for Nilda did not obscure the irony that the two drug addicts who came to the ER threatening suicide—with almost certainly no intention of either killing themselves or challenging their addiction—were directly admitted to inpatient beds. And this irony does not hide the paradox that someone who was disabled by a stroke after using cocaine, and then stayed clean for five years, went back to using that drug.

Bipolar Depression
The World Too Low Down

Like the Roman god Janus, who had two faces and could look both forward and backward, someone with bipolar disorder looks out at the world with an exaggerated emotionality that, at different times, can point down (depressive face) or up (manic face). Many bipolar patients have long periods when their symptoms are under good control or are absent. Relapses are often precipitated by stress. Patients may stop taking medication after a period of stability because they feel "cured" (almost always a false notion for someone with a real bipolar diagnosis), not crediting the medication for a symptom-free interval. Or the side effects of medication may become so bothersome that the patient focuses exclusively on eliminating this discomfort, even when going off medication in the past has led to relapse.

Bipolar patients—formerly called manic depressives—frequently come to the ER with extremes of low or high mood they cannot manage. The bottom may have dropped out of their lives, and depression may bring on a despairing paralysis. These patients are often at high risk for suicide.

"I'm sorry that I have hurt you—but it's time to draw things to a close—to end my misery. I have hurt a lot of people and hurting Pam was the last straw. I have hurt you both, and 2 people & 3 animals died because of me [Jeff's mother told me what happened with one of the animals, but I cannot recall]. I have no course but to end this suffering. Please know I love you, and I'm sorry—Please tell Pam that this was the only way—and that I loved her in spite of my behavior."

Around 4 p.m., Jeff parked his car in the driveway of the house where Pam, his ex-girlfriend, had an apartment. He inserted a piece of plastic tubing he had bought earlier that day into the tailpipe and fastened it in place with string. He put the other end of the tubing through the opening between the top edge of the window and the door frame and raised the window sufficiently to hold the tubing against the frame. He started the engine. Twenty minutes later, a neighbor saw what was happening and flagged down a passing motorist, who then brought Jeff, willingly, to the ER.

"I tried to kill myself," Jeff, 26, told me at the start of the interview. But he showed no signs of carbon monoxide poisoning in the ER. His oxyhemoglobin was 100 percent, suggesting that he had taken in little or none of this lethal gas. Even small amounts of carbon monoxide cause confusion and memory loss, as well as problems with coordination. Jeff had none of these deficits. He knew who he was, where he was, the date, and the season. He answered all questions quickly and crisply. There were no signs of memory impairment.

Asked to describe his mood, Jeff said that he was "extremely depressed and anxious." A difficult relationship with his girlfriend, Pam, who was considerably older (39), had ended three months before at her insistence. He had been depressed since then and had become more depressed during the last two weeks. Jeff seemed beside himself, so preoccupied with the loss of Pam that he could attend to nothing else. His sleep was down to a few hours a night, and his appetite was off. He had thoughts that he would be better off dead, and he conceived and followed through on a plan that could have ended his life.

Jeff first had psychiatric help around age five, following what he described as "violent outbursts in school." This disinhibited behavior appeared to have been an expression of inner conflict and did not result in injury to others. He had additional counseling and therapy on and off since then but was never admitted to a psychiatric hospital.

In 1991, Jeff graduated from a prestigious university, where he had majored in English and Spanish. He had worked as a telecommunications analyst for that university until three months before he came to the ER but was currently unemployed. He never married and had no children. Jeff was born with nerve damage to both ears, and he wore two hearing aids. He had a history of prostatitis but was otherwise in good health. His most striking feature was a head that was slightly too large for a rather short body.

"I'm addicted to the girls I go out with," he told me. "I go into withdrawal when they are not around." Complicating the matter further, he considered Pam "the only person for me." He used the words "ruminate," "obsess," and "fixation" while telling me how he was handling his loss. I called Pam to get her perspective. She was tearful and obviously frightened. She and Jeff had known each other for three years. "He's a nice person, but he does crazy things," she told me. She described an incident when Jeff served alcohol to a 16-year-old girl, who became so intoxicated that she had to be taken to the ER. Pam said he had been involved with other underage girls. After Pam broke off their relationship, Jeff, continuing to pursue her, showed up at her job and at the university where she was taking classes (he was officially barred from the campus by the administration). Pam's last words to me on the phone were, "Please tell him to leave me alone."

About an hour later, Pam came to the ER with two letters he had written her; there had been four in the last five days. One read in part, "So, I probably would never have left you, and that would not have been right for either of us. You always said that I should have someone my own age [Pam was 13 years older] with similar interests, but I came to believe, unfortunately, that you were the only one for me. I became addicted to you and struggled with that every day. I could not love you, live with you as I did, and expect you not to feel anger or betrayal at some things I did." The tone of both letters, as reflected in this excerpt, was muted desperation bordering on despair.

During our phone conversation, Pam told me that in 1989 Jeff, driving on a busy street at night, struck and killed two pedestrians who walked in front of his car. He had not been driving fast (a fact substantiated by someone who witnessed the accident) or drinking alcohol. The police considered the pedestrians to have been jaywalking, and Jeff was judged not to be at fault and was not charged. But he felt hugely guilty nonetheless. Several days before he tried to asphyxiate himself, he visited the graveyard where the two persons who had died were buried. Pam, who went with him, said he addressed their tombstones and asked for forgiveness.

Jeff did not receive therapy for the emotional trauma he suffered after the accident until five years later. He told me that the psychologist with whom he was currently working refused to discuss the accident or its effect on him, saying they would "get around to that eventually." Meanwhile, according to Jeff's parents, who came to the ER, he had become more depressed during the last four years. His grandfather, to whom he had been close, died in 1990, and this loss still haunted him.

Jeff was also in financial trouble. His mother said he "owed $50,000 to the stock market," but did not specify to whom this money was owed. Jeff's depression had deepened still further during the last few months, and he had talked about taking his life. What appeared to be a suicide note to his mother and father was attached to his chart. It was printed on a plain sheet of typewriter paper.

> Dear Mom and Dad,
>
> I'm sorry that I have hurt you—but it's time to draw things to a close—to end my misery. I have hurt a lot of people and hurting Pam was the last straw. I have hurt you both, and 2 people & 3 animals died because of me [Jeff's mother told me what happened with one of the animals, but I cannot recall]. I have no course but to end this suffering. Please know I love you, and I'm sorry—Please tell Pam that this was the only way— and that I loved her in spite of my behavior.
>
> Jeff

Jeff's note can be read as a statement of despair. But being in despair does not necessarily signify an intent or determination to end one's life, even though doing so would end one's problems. During the interview, Jeff acknowledged having had earlier passive suicidal thoughts, but he denied planning or trying to hurt himself before the day he came to the ER. While the asphyxiation attempt had lethal potential, he had chosen a time and a place that made it highly likely he would be discovered and stopped.

Jeff told me that he had been considered "borderline manic depressive" by his doctors for many years and had had "mixed episodes" when mood rapidly changed from sadness, to irritability, to euphoria, and back again. He denied ever having had psychotic symptoms, either when manic or severely depressed. He never abused drugs or alcohol, eliminating this common complication in the diagnosis of his mood disorder. Jeff was diagnosed with full-blown bipolar disorder early in 1996. His mother, as well as a grandparent on each side of the family, was also diagnosed with bipolar disorder. Jeff was started on lithium but did not do well on this medication. With high doses he felt nauseated and vomited. With lower doses there was no response. He was then prescribed Depakote and Klonopin but never took these medications.

Jeff told me he had manic episodes lasting up to two weeks. His most recent episode had occurred several weeks earlier and went on for two days. When manic, Jeff could go for several days without sleep and not feel tired. His thoughts raced: "I can't hold an idea long when I'm manic." He became hypersexual: "I have so much sexual energy to be released." When manic, he overestimated his capabilities and became boastful. Jeff also spent himself into debt during manic episodes. "He has no idea of the magnitude of the [financial] situation he is in," his mother told me, implying that his judgment was poor even when his mood was relatively normal. She added that when manic, and sometimes during mixed episodes, "he has no remorse for any kind of behavior." Jeff did not tell me that he was $50,000 in debt, but he did mention, with some pride, that he had *made* money in the stock market. According to his mother, Jeff was helping Pam with her expenses in spite of being in debt.

As happens to most people with bipolar disorder, the behavioral disinhibition that occurred when Jeff was manic contributed sooner or later to the next cycle of his depression. The world does not tolerate for long the excesses of behavior at the upper extreme of mood. Reality, averted here, must eventually be faced; the piper must be paid. Jeff was now at a loss to work his way out of the hole he had been digging for himself for so long. His life was at a low point and out of control. For the first time, in spite of many earlier ups and downs, he seriously considered ending it. Jeff felt it was not "safe" for him to go home. He signed himself into the psychiatric unit.

The course over time of any mental illness is difficult to predict. But considering the natural history of bipolar disorder, as well as Jeff's family history of the illness and his worsening symptoms, it appears that this young man could be in for a difficult time.

8   Bipolar Mania
The World Too High Up

During manic episodes, patients may feel as if the lid has come off their lives. They often lose their judgment and get into trouble because their behavior is out of control. They may feel "great" during this time, but the feeling does not last. Untreated, the artificial, physiologically induced high of mania always gives way to another episode of depression. When patients become manic beyond a certain point, they may have psychotic symptoms and act like schizophrenic patients in relapse.

As I explained why I felt she needed to be hospitalized, Dora's "happy" mania changed to something quite different. She became agitated, loud, angry, and obscene (the explicitness here was clearly different from the hypersexuality displayed earlier in the interview). Her friendliness turned into accusation, and I was now the cause of her trouble.

Working shifts in the ER, the odds are against any one clinician getting to evaluate a bipolar patient at the opposite extremes of emotional decompensation—the best way to see both "faces" of this mental disorder. I was not asked to interview Jeff again, and his manic side was forever lost to me. I have chosen another patient, Dora, to show the bipolar's "up face," because she came to the ER with a florid and classic manic exacerbation of her chronic bipolar illness.

Dora, 41, was brought to the ER by the police on emergency petition taken out by her father: "Dora is hallucinating and not acting in the proper manner—making statements which are not true. She is not taking her medication as prescribed." Dora insisted she was taking her Navane, Benadryl, and Depakote and seemed not to understand why she had been brought to the ER. She was doing her best to put a normal face on her situation. But as hard as she tried to keep a lid on her mania, her restlessness and rapid speech, along with her tendency to veer off course in her conversation, convinced me that she was in a state of manic decompensation.

Dora had been diagnosed with bipolar disorder at age 21 and was on disability. She had been hospitalized many times, including one long stay at a state hospital. Her last inpatient treatment was less than a year earlier. For the last five years, she had been followed by a local university hospital's mobile treatment team.

During the first part of the interview, Dora stayed on the "happy" side of mania. She seemed eager to participate in the dialogue required for the evaluation. She was friendly, was patient with the interview process, and showed no trace of irritability, a common sign of dysphoric ("unhappy") mania. Her appearance belied her decompensation. She was neatly dressed in a striped shirt and black pants. Her hair was covered with a well-tied bandanna. She carried a stylish black handbag.

Dora had never married but had a six-year-old son, who was cared for by a family member. Dora finished high school and had her own apartment. She denied ever using illicit drugs or abusing alcohol. Her toxicology screen was negative.

Dora knew who she was, where she was, and the exact date. Her memory for recent and distant events seemed intact. She appeared incredulous that her father had taken out the emergency petition. "Why am I here?" she asked more than once, indicating either poor insight into her condition or a willful disregard of that condition.

Dora's speech was excessive, loud, pressured, and rapid. She would start to answer a question, then suddenly go to another, unrelated topic as if something were driving her off her initial train of thought. Our dialogue was dominated by her intense, pressured production of wordy speech. Often, it seemed that, if I hadn't stopped her at some point, she would have continued indefinitely on a subject I had not introduced. In the language of psychiatry, Dora's speech was "circumstantial"; she could not answer a question directly and had to be interrupted repeatedly to bring her back to the subject until she gave me the information I needed.

Dora emphatically denied ever hearing voices she felt came from inside her head (auditory hallucinations), or seeing things another person with her at the time could not see (visual hallucinations). She also denied ever having tried to harm herself in the past or wanting to do so now. She claimed to be sleeping and eating normally. Undoubtedly, her father would have been able to supply details of her decompensated behavior beyond the sketchy facts given in the emergency petition, but I was not able to contact him. I would have been particularly interested in knowing what he meant when he said she was "hallucinating."

Throughout the interview, as often happens with bipolar patients during a manic phase, Dora showed signs of hypersexuality. She informed me that a visible part of my anatomy pleased her and speculated that a part not visible probably would. Using the most graphic terms, she described how her boyfriend had oral sex with other women. Dora also spoke explicitly about her own genitalia. The language was of the kind Xaviera Hollander favors in her *Penthouse* magazine column.

Dora clearly needed an inpatient stay to get back on medication and stabilize this latest manic exacerbation of her chronic illness. But she did not see it that way—according to her, nothing was wrong. She was taking her medication; she was not ill; her father had overreacted in having her brought to the ER; and she wanted to go home.

As I explained why I felt she needed to be hospitalized, Dora's "happy" mania changed to something quite different. She became agitated, loud, angry, and obscene (the explicitness here was clearly different from the hypersexuality displayed earlier in the interview). Her friendliness turned into accusation, and I was now the cause of her trouble. Dora left the interview room and paced restlessly in the hallway outside my office. As she approached me in a threatening way, the black handbag I had seen earlier as "stylish" now swung hard by its strap in my direction. I backed into my office and closed the door just in time to miss its sting.

With the help of several nurses and a technician, Dora was talked back into the interview room and given an injection of Inapsine. She became calmer and more rational. I explained again why I felt she could not go home and needed to spend some time in our psychiatric unit. Her main fear seemed to be that she would be hospitalized for an extended period, as had happened at least once before in a state hospital. I told her that, if she did not sign herself in voluntarily, she would be committed. Like most patients given this choice, she signed the voluntary admission form, though resentfully. She waited restlessly for an attendant to escort her upstairs to the psychiatric unit.

Dora had a rocky three-week stay in the unit. Nursing notes for her second hospital day stated that she was angry, hostile, moody, restless, irritable, distractable, and disagreeable. She asked to be discharged almost as soon as she was admitted, consistent with her insistence in the ER that she was not ill and did not need help. She demanded that she be allowed to smoke, a privilege not given to Level 1 patients (who may not leave the unit). Dora denied hearing voices but continued to have pressured speech. She had difficulty with sleep, sleeping only two or three hours on some nights. The dosage of Depakote was increased; Prolixin, Benadryl, and Valium were added. During the first few days of her hospitalization, when she became agitated and threatening, she was also given injections of Inapsine, the tranquilizer that had helped calm her in the ER.

After nine days, Dora was advanced to Level 2 (patients may leave the unit with staff members and smoke with their permission), though she was still periodically agitated, had pressured speech, and did not always follow the rules. A nursing note for her 11th hospital day included these remarks: "The patient has been irritable for long periods, very easily frustrated, and appears to have minimal coping skills when needs are not met immediately. [She] readily resorts to threats and quickly escalates to the verge of verbal abuse. [She] continues to be loud and intrusive, but [is] redirectable. Escorted off the unit for a Level 2 walk, and she was appropriate." Dora still had problems sleeping. She insisted that, after she was discharged from the hospital, she would not work anymore with the mobile treatment team that had followed her for the last five years.

Dora continued to deny she was ill but did take her medication as prescribed. She pressed the staff about being discharged and asked to be advanced to Level 3 (patients are allowed to go off the unit by themselves, as long as they do not leave the hospital building, and may smoke in areas where smoking is allowed). On her 16th hospital day, a nursing note recorded that she was "cooperative and calm," though her speech was still pressured at times. Three days later, her attending psychiatrist wrote in the chart, "The patient is stable enough in mood to be Level 3, while discharge planning continues." He added that he considered this manic exacerbation of her chronic bipolar illness to be "in remission." The following day, a nurse noted, "The patient has been less manic and has done a good job maintaining calm behavior." A day after that, Dora seemed to be holding on to her gains: "The patient continues to be stable in her hypomania." Curiously, there was no mention anywhere in the chart of the hypersexual behavior I had seen in the ER.

Dora's three-week rocky road back from her acute mania is fairly typical of what it takes to bring such an episode under control. Schizophrenic patients in relapse, either because of increased stress, noncompliance with medication, or both, can often be stabilized, even if they are psychotic, after a few days in the hospital. But the mania and depression that are the two (Janus) faces of decompensated bipolar disorder are frequently more intractable states, requiring a longer stay and greater effort from staff members overseeing their treatment.

Schizophrenia

Being Unable to Share a World with Others

Known as "the cancer of mental illness," schizophrenia can core a life. Often, someone with chronic schizophrenia loses the capacity to cue into the basic signals of the everyday world. These signals are so fundamental that they would not be explicitly recognized as constituents of the social order by most people who do not have the illness. The bizarreness that schizophrenics often show may be due as much to a lack of relatedness to others and the world that is rooted in this flaw as it is to the more obvious psychic perturbations caused by delusions and hallucinations.

For schizophrenic patients, the most common symptoms of relapse are auditory and visual hallucinations, delusions, bizarre and sometimes violent behavior, paranoia, and insomnia. Other symptoms frequently seen are decreased social interaction, poor hygiene, apathy, and the inability to attend to the basic tasks of daily living.

Kim told me she had stopped taking her medication because she had died in the recent fire that damaged her house, had been reborn with a new body and a new head, and so no longer needed to take the medication that her former body required.

Of all the schizophrenic patients I evaluated in the ER, I have elected to tell Kim's story because her illness shows what this most devastating of psychiatric disorders can do to a person: how someone once healthy and highly functional can, during the gravest exacerbations of the illness, be reduced to thoughts, feelings, and behaviors that are barely recognizable as human.

Kim was brought to the ER late one evening by the police on emergency petition. Several weeks earlier, the house she lived in and owned had been damaged by a fire caused by an electrical short. It was October, but Kim had been living in the house without electricity, heat, hot water, or phone service. Earlier that evening, a neighbor who knew of Kim's chronic mental illness and had observed her during periods of relapse, noticed a candle burning in a darkened window. Thinking that the open flame might lead to another fire, the neighbor called the police.

Kim, 38, was born in the United States to Chinese parents, who returned to Taiwan after her father finished his medical training; Kim and her siblings remained in the United States. She graduated from a prestigious women's college and earned a master's degree in human development. Her marriage to an Oriental man ended in divorce; there were no children. She had not been employed for some time.

Kim was first hospitalized at age 26 with what was then diagnosed as a psychotic mood disorder. It is not clear when the schizophrenia diagnosis was made. The records available to us did not provide any information about the early course of her illness but noted hospitalizations in 1992 and 1994, as well as admissions to this hospital in May and August 1995.

When I entered the room to begin the evaluation, Kim was sitting on a gurney with a sheet pulled up around her. Her appearance belied what she was soon to reveal about herself. She was short, with a well-developed body, and had dark, shoulder-length hair that was well cared for. This attractive young woman was in no apparent distress and would have stood out in a crowd only for being attractive.

Kim knew who she was, where she was, and the date. Asked about her mood, she replied that she felt "fine" and denied being depressed. She also denied having any intention or plan to hurt herself. The chart records did not allude to any past suicide attempt. Kim had no significant medical history or any current medical problems, and she did not abuse drugs or alcohol.

Kim told me she had stopped taking her medication because she had died in the recent fire that damaged her house, had been reborn with a new body and a new head, and so no longer needed to take the medication that her former body required (she was not injured in the fire). Kim told me that God spoke to her directly, but she did not offer any further details. "I can see Europe," she said. "I have very different eyes." Her answers to even the simplest questions revealed strong underlying psychotic processes. "I am an Oriental woman. I eat and I shit. I don't know about American women." I cannot recall what question I might have asked to elicit that response.

I contacted the psychiatrist who had been following Kim for some time. He pointed out that her behavior in the ER was not very different from her recent baseline behavior. None of the neuroleptic and atypical antipsychotic medications tried, including Prolixin, Trilafon, Orap, Risperdal, and Clozaril had benefited her significantly. Lithium was added to some of these neuroleptics and atypicals, but with little effect. After her recent hospitalizations, Kim had been quick to go off whatever medication she had started on. The reason she gave me for doing so this last time was clearly delusional.

Kim had not noticeably responded to individual psychotherapy or benefited from the therapeutic opportunities offered by her most recent hospital stays. She seemed to have been drawn into a fragmented world that no intervention had any power to draw her out of. In spite of her obvious psychotic state, Kim's psychiatrist felt it was doubtful she would benefit from being admitted now. (She had come to the ER solely on a neighbor's assumption that a lighted candle in a house without electricity portended danger.) The psychiatrist felt that she could be discharged and agreed to see her the next morning. He planned to resume her medication.

A man claiming to be Kim's boyfriend came to the ER and volunteered to escort her home. He told us he was negotiating with the insurance company on Kim's behalf for a settlement on the fire damage to her house and was making arrangements with contractors to have the repairs made. However, a notation in Kim's chart raised questions about this man's integrity and stated there was reason to believe that he had already stolen $23,000 from her.

Three weeks after I discharged Kim from the ER, she was admitted to the inpatient psychiatric unit. She was admitted again five weeks later, and eight weeks after that, and 12 weeks after that. Clearly, she was noncompliant with treatment. Following each discharge from the hospital, she would stop taking the medication that was resumed.

The records showed that Kim was more grossly psychotic during these hospital stays than when I evaluated her in the ER. More withdrawn. More disorganized. More thought-disordered. More delusional. More hallucinatory. These delusional statements, recorded in the chart, were attributed to Kim during her four admissions to our inpatient psychiatric unit that followed in close order after my ER evaluation: "I'm so superior to everyone"; "George Bush keeps running into my house"; "God was downstairs in my house"; "I am a Jew" [her chart notes she is Presbyterian]; "The Virgin Mary doesn't need electricity, heat, or phone service because she lives on a higher plane"; and "I am the Virgin Mary." After this last statement she added, "The one thing I really enjoy is sex." On one admission to our psychiatric unit, Kim had a positive pregnancy test; she had an abortion shortly after.

While hospitalized, Kim also reported these hallucinations: "God touched me in my sleep"; "Jesus told me I'm his mother"; and "I have communications with Joseph, and he tells me I'm his wife."

Kim was seen begging her neighbors for food. It was clear that she could no longer take care of herself. Adult Protective Services was called to investigate, and the inpatient unit asked them to look into the possibly exploitive relationship between Kim and her "boyfriend." Other instances of Kim's disorganized behavior documented in her chart include her planting flowers in neighbors' gardens (without being asked to do so) and running nude through the alleys of her neighborhood.

During her last admission to our hospital, Kim was restarted on Clozaril. She remained grossly psychotic, delusional, and thought-disordered. The staff felt that she needed intensive, long-term inpatient treatment, and she was transferred to a state mental hospital.

Alzheimer's Dementia

The World Dissolves as the
Glue of Memory Cracks

Alzheimer's disease damages the biological substrate of mental processes, and eventually of physical functions as well. The first symptoms are memory loss, confusion, and disorientation. Later, the capacity to perform even the most basic physical acts is compromised, then lost altogether. The disorder usually begins in late middle life (but sometimes earlier or later) and is fatal within five to 10 years.

Most patients with Alzheimer's who come to the ER have already been diagnosed. They are usually brought in because of a sudden worsening of their condition. They may wander away from their home or treatment facility, or a behavioral outburst may have frightened someone responsible for their care. Occasionally, particularly when the patient and the family have denied the obvious signs and symptoms, the Alzheimer's diagnosis is made in the ER.

I was struck by what was still left of this sweet lady's demented brain and mind—which did not know the year, season, month, or day—that made her want to attempt these last acts of courtesy before leaving the ER.

I can still vividly picture this 79-year-old woman, a retired grade-school teacher, who was brought to the ER from a foster home by her case manager. In an unprecedented outburst earlier that day, she had become agitated and accused others at the home of trying to hurt her. Ida had been diagnosed with Alzheimer's disease. She had lived with a 16-year-old granddaughter until the young woman could no longer provide the care she needed. Ida was then placed in foster care by Adult Protective Services. According to the case manager, who had worked with her for six months, Ida had done well until the day she was brought to the ER.

Except for hypertension, Ida's physical health was good. Nifedi-pine was prescribed, but she had not taken this medication for some time. Ida's appearance belied the dementia that was so obviously con-suming her. She wore a print dress that hung well on a body that could have been 20 years younger. Her hair had been recently done. Though her affect was blunted, Ida's face had no major creases and still showed some of the light that usually leaves the faces of the de-mented. And, unlike other patients with dementia I have evaluated, she still seemed aware of her surroundings, as if something in her was trying to hold on to the world outside.

As soon as I began to talk to this woman, it was clear that she was ter-ribly compromised. Ida could not recall the outburst that had brought her to the ER, though she did not deny it. She could not recall the name of the grammar school where she had taught for many years. "My re-membrance is bad," she said with an understatement that she did not seem to comprehend. Ida did not know the year, the season, the month, or the date. She did not know what state, county, or town she was in. She did not know that she was in a hospital or what floor of the building she was on. Ida could name three simple objects but could not recall them a minute later. She could not subtract 7 from 100, and she could not spell *world* backwards. She did identify a pencil and a watch when these objects were shown to her.

Ida could not repeat the sentence, "No ifs, ands, or buts." She was able to follow the three-stage verbal command, "Take a paper in your right hand, fold it in half, and put it on the floor." She could also respond to the written command, "Close your eyes." Asked to write a sentence, she produced, "Tomorrow is Sunday" (it was Friday). Asked to copy a drawing of two intersecting pentagons, she drew a complex figure that did not at all resemble the figure shown to her. These questions were from the Mini-Mental Status Examination. Her score was 7 out of 30.

Ida gave little information during the interview, though she showed every sign of wanting to cooperate. She seemed to lack the resources necessary to grasp and process many of the questions. She did acknowl-edge having been depressed in the past but denied current depression.

Ida denied any intention or plan to harm herself or anyone else, as well as any attempt to harm herself in the past. The case manager filled in many of the details required to finish the evaluation. She reported that Ida had lost a significant amount of weight during the last two years and recently had trouble sleeping. Before coming under the aegis of Adult Protective Services, Ida had turned on the gas stove in her home without lighting it. While living with her granddaughter, she pulled cords from electrical appliances out of the wall sockets.

The case manager contacted the foster home, and they agreed to take Ida back. Ida was willing to go back. But it occurred to me that she may have reached the point in her progressive dementing illness where it was becoming impossible for her to cope with the people who made up her milieu—and for them to cope with her. I wondered how long it would be before Ida would need a higher level of care. Earlier that day, her physician had given her a prescription for Haldol, but she had not started taking this medication.

When I went to say good-bye, Ida was straightening the sheet and flattening out the pillow on the gurney where she had been placed prior to the interview. She was collecting used Styrofoam cups and wrappers from the food she and the case manager had been served. She was trying to put this refuse into a trash container that was covered with a metal lid controlled by a foot pedal. Finding it hard to complete this simple task, Ida seemed genuinely perplexed by the difficulty she was having. I was struck by what was still left of this sweet lady's demented brain and mind—which did not know the year, season, month, or day—that made her want to attempt these last acts of courtesy before leaving the ER.

The neurologist Oliver Sacks observed a similar conservation of function in his demented patients. Writing about Willem de Kooning's painting during the last 15 years of the artist's life, when he had Alzheimer's, Sacks wagered, "'Style,' neurologically, is the deepest part of one's being, and may be preserved, almost to the last, in a dementia." I sensed that Ida, by tidying up her room, was showing me the last of her style.

Part II

Complex Stories

These are stories about patients with more complex psychopathology. In one story, two mental disorders drove a woman's unhappiness and dysfunction. In another, a wrong diagnosis given years earlier made it all but impossible for a woman to engage the real issues underlying her mental illness.

11 Panic Disorder Fed by Emotional Dependence

Panic disorder originates in anxiety. Depending on basic personality structure, one person may survive a difficult and traumatic situation relatively unharmed (though not necessarily unchanged), while another goes on to have crippling symptoms of panic. In the terminology of *DSM-IV,* this interrelatedness of personality, negative experience, and mental disorder can be thought of as the pathology of Axis II driving the pathology of Axis I.

Those with a dependent personality show a persistent and excessive need to be taken care of that leads to submissive and clinging behavior, as well as fears of separation. Intuitively, it seems that, in the face of negative life experiences that challenge a fragile identity, someone with such a personality structure and associated dynamics would be predisposed to anxiety and to developing the symptoms of panic disorder.

I tried to get Robyn to focus on what she was getting from her involvement with Erik. At first, she insisted that she wasn't getting anything positive, and was just being hurt. After I challenged her denial, she came up with this: "I gave Erik so much of myself I felt I had to get him back to get myself back." A classic answer from a classic dependent personality, I thought. The boundaries between herself and the man she depended on hardly existed.

By the time I interviewed Robyn, her panic attack had all but passed. But this 21-year-old woman was still shaken and tearful. This was her first panic attack, and she did not know what had hit her. She thought she was having a heart attack.

Robyn had gone out the evening before, a Saturday evening, drunk four or five mixed drinks, and returned home around 6:30 a.m. After two hours of sleep, she woke up hyperventilating and had a tight feeling in her chest. Her fingers and feet were numb and tingling. She experienced what she called a "closing in feeling." Robyn thought she was going to die. These symptoms disappeared, but she had another similar episode later that day. Her father brought her to the ER.

Robyn's appetite had increased recently, and she was eating more and gaining weight. She was also waking up in the middle of the night. Her friends interested her less. She acknowledged a certain dysphoria but denied being seriously depressed or feeling hopeless. Robyn denied having any thought or plan to hurt herself, or having ever made any attempts to do so. Recalling how hard it had been to breathe during her recent panic attacks, she assured me, "I'm afraid of dying." Robyn saw herself as a social drinker but did not feel that she abused alcohol. (One might wonder about the four or five mixed drinks she had had the night before she came to the ER.) She had been using marijuana on and off for several months.

I had seen Robyn in the ER five months earlier. "I hate myself, and I'm very angry," she told me at the top of that interview. Her anger was diffusely focused, which probably accounted for why so much of it was self-directed; she had been throwing herself against the wall at home. Her mother, who had brought her to the ER and was present during the interview, volunteered that Robyn had bruises all over her body and was also pulling out her hair. "Everything is my fault," she said as if convinced. During that first interview, Robyn's speech was tearful and plaintive. Her affect was restricted, though not flat. She looked away as she spoke to me and often stared at the floor. When I asked her about this, she said she frequently avoided eye contact while talking to people and thought that low self-esteem was the reason.

Robyn had felt well until three weeks earlier. But then she became depressed, could not enjoy what she usually enjoyed, had problems concentrating, and took several days off from her assembly-line job at a factory. She felt hopeless and had thoughts about dying but was not thinking of harming herself. Her sleep was down to three or four hours a night instead of the usual eight. She denied any psychotic symptoms, and I saw no evidence of psychosis during the interview. The diagnosis for this first ER visit was adjustment disorder with anxiety and depressed mood. Robyn had no psychiatric history or significant medical problems. She took Naprosyn for menstrual pains and had been on the appetite suppressant phentermine for two months (she was slightly overweight). She reported using marijuana for the first time about a week earlier and had smoked eight to 10 joints since then. Her toxicology screen was positive for cannabinoids and amphetamines.

Robyn told me that her father had verbally abused her since she was a child. A week before, they had had a serious disagreement at a family outing. She had just broken up with her boyfriend of three years, Erik, a heavy drug user who also sold drugs. "He's not good for me," she said. "He's ruined his life, and now he's ruining mine." Still, Robyn could not let go of Erik emotionally. "I still love him, but I don't like the person he is," she reported as if the contradiction could not be resolved. This young man insisted that she pay for everything when they were out together and often played her off against other women.

Clearly, Robyn needed intensive work with an outpatient psychotherapist. We worked together for two months, first weekly, then biweekly. Her physician prescribed Zoloft and Ativan. A psychiatrist she saw later switched her to Prozac. Though she had no side effects, Robyn stopped the Prozac after two days but continued taking Ativan for several weeks. It seemed ironic that someone so dependent on others for her most basic needs would defy a doctor's medication order. This 21-year-old woman did not have a driver's license and had never tried to get one. Her mother drove her to my office for our sessions.

We quickly identified the issues that made Robyn so vulnerable to anxiety and depression. Her story was redolent of Axis II and reverberated with the elements of dependent personality disorder. The *DSM-IV* defines this pathology as "a pervasive and excessive need to be taken care of that leads to submissive and clinging behavior." Five of the following eight criteria are required for the diagnosis:

1. Difficulty making everyday decisions without an excessive amount of advice and reassurance from others.
2. Needs others to assume responsibility for most major areas of his or her life.
3. Difficulty expressing disagreement with others because of fear of loss of support or approval.
4. Difficulty initiating projects or doing things on his or her own (because of a lack of self-confidence in judgment or abilities rather than a lack of motivation or energy).
5. Goes to excessive lengths to obtain nurturance and support from others, to the point of volunteering to do things that are unpleasant.
6. Feels uncomfortable or helpless when alone because of exaggerated fears of being unable to care for himself or herself.
7. Urgently seeks another relationship as a source of care and support when a close relationship ends.
8. Is unrealistically preoccupied with fears of being left to take care of himself or herself.

Robyn met all eight criteria, some more strikingly than others. Her Millon Clinical Multiaxial Inventory–II (a test for personality disorders) showed very high scores on the avoidant, dependent, passive-aggressive, self-defeating, and debasement scales. She was bruised from throwing herself against the wall, and she also pulled out her hair. Someone with this personality structure and the associated dynamics would be expected to have a fragile identity. Faced with recent negative experiences, it seems likely that Robyn's brittle self—another way of expressing a fragile identity—might have been sufficiently challenged to produce symptoms of anxiety and depression. In the parlance of the *DSM-IV*, this could be thought of as Axis II pathology driving Axis I pathology.

In our sessions, we clarified how Robyn's acceptance of her father's lifelong verbal and emotional abuse had predisposed her to dependent and abusive involvements with others, including Erik. "My father treated me this way," she said, "and I guess I expected other people to act that way." Robyn seemed to make rapid and steady progress. At what turned out to be our last session, she said, "There's a piece of me that fights back [now]. I feel alive. Before, I felt like I was dead." Robyn did not keep her next scheduled appointment. When I called, she said she thought we had done as much work as needed. "I'm fine, real good," she insisted. "Everything is fine." I had my doubts about how long things would stay "fine" and told her to call me if she felt she needed further help.

I did not see or hear from Robyn until three months later, on a Sunday evening, when she reappeared in the ER, frightened in the aftermath of her first panic attack. It did not take long to identify the reasons for her severe anxiety. Three weeks earlier, Robyn had resumed her sexual relationship with Erik. "He was nice at first," she said. "Then he was like he was before. . . . It should not have happened. But I was in more control than before. . . . I recognized what I was doing. I didn't deny it." Robyn told me she would rather be hurt by someone whose pattern of abuse she knew than take a chance on being hurt by someone else.

Robyn had worked in a factory until two weeks before this second ER visit. During a discussion about her work with two supervisors, she became argumentative and slapped them both in the face—another paradoxical act for someone with a dependent personality. She was unceremoniously fired, after having performed well in that job for two years. Unemployed now, she found her bills piling up. Robyn was spending money she did not have, maxing out a $500 Montgomery Ward card and an $800 Sears card, buying presents for herself and others. Her attitude about money had drastically changed. "I've been working since I was 15," she said. "I've always had money." Now she didn't, and she was accumulating a large debt.

Robyn's grandmother was in the hospital recuperating from hip-replacement surgery. Robyn had been living with her grandmother for some time and looked to this strong woman for emotional support and affirmation. Though she got along well with her mother, Robyn had left home to get away from her emotionally abusive father and did not feel comfortable there. Her grandfather had died of cancer five years earlier. "He held everything together," she said with urgency. "He brought a lot of love to us. He was the first person I ever lost. I could never accept the fact that he was gone. I'm still coming to terms."

These new developments seemed likely reasons for Robyn's severe anxiety and the breakthrough of that anxiety as panic attacks. Renewing a relationship with an abusive man, being unemployed and having financial trouble for the first time, and then seeing her grandmother laid up in the hospital (which almost surely reactivated unresolved feelings for her dead grandfather) must have threatened much of what this young woman felt was stable and worthwhile in her life. With her dependent personality, how could Robyn's world still seem even a minimally familiar or safe place?

We resumed therapy. Robyn's physician started her again on Zoloft and Ativan. Robyn had several more panic attacks during the time we worked together (a sufficient number for the diagnosis of panic disorder; see chapter 2), but none as severe as the episode that brought her to the ER the second time. She described one attack as "feeling like my whole body was on fire. . . . I was in a whole different world." I tried to get Robyn to focus on what she was getting from her involvement with Erik. At first, she insisted that she wasn't getting anything positive and was just being hurt. After I challenged her denial, she came up with this: "I gave Erik so much of myself I felt I had to get him back to get myself back." A classic answer from a classic dependent personality, I thought. The boundaries between herself and the man she depended on hardly existed.

What was Robyn getting from this entirely inappropriate man? Most obviously, companionship, a twisted kind of affirmation, and sex. I helped her to acknowledge that her involvement with Erik was not just a passive acceptance of the little he was doling out to her, but an ongoing choice she made day by day to accept it. All through our second go at therapy, Robyn kept insisting that things were not as bad for her as when we worked together the first time. After about a month, she showed what seemed like real improvement. She made a clean break with Erik, though she still thought about him a good deal, even after he was jailed on drug charges and theft. She found a part-time job as a cashier. Her physician increased the dosage of Zoloft, and Robyn took herself off Ativan because she felt she did not need it.

I encouraged Robyn to elaborate on her feelings about the abusive man she had just ditched. Comments like "bad news," "no future," and "the lowest person in the world" rang true. "My investment in him was counterfeit. . . . I went bankrupt." But she made it clear that, though she knew Erik was wrong for her, she still had "strong feelings" for him. "Erik cared about me once," she maintained, probably recalling the brief periods when he had been "nice"—which he no doubt was when he was setting her up.

Robyn was still clinging to Erik's affirmation. Gradually, though, she came to see what this had cost her. The dependent person gladly pays a heavy price for a little affirmation—up to a point. Robyn was starting to get beyond that point now. "Erik was the best thing that happened to me this year; and he was the worst thing," she said, convincing me that she was beginning to recognize her ambivalence about this man. It seemed she was just where she needed to be to work through the painful dilemma of having loved someone who did not deserve love and could not return it.

The full-blown panic attacks stopped, then the chest pain and shortness of breath, the last somatic conversion symptoms of her anxiety. Robyn's sleep, fitful and interrupted since her first panic attack, increased to six hours a night. She looked and sounded better.

And she met a new man. He was 26, had an infant son, and was getting a divorce. She talked as if this relationship might have some future. "I'm giving and I'm getting," she told me. "I'm smiling and being smiled back at."

Our second round of therapy lasted two months, as had the first. Again, Robyn did not keep her last appointment. She called the office and left a message that she was doing well. I was more persuaded this time, though I knew that her personality must still be dominated by the structure and dynamics of dependence. How far Robyn goes beyond this pathological state will turn, in part, on how vigorously she rejects that mode as a way of life and on what kind of luck she has finding other people—particularly men—who will treat her fairly. Of course, even the fairest of relationships eventually becomes conflicted (and less fair), and during these times it will be difficult for Robyn to hold on to her sense of self-worth and act autonomously. Robyn most likely will always have a certain deficit of self that leaves her feeling she is not worthy of the best this world has to offer.

Histrionics Mistaken for Schizophrenia

The ER may be the best—or worst—place to diagnose a psychiatric disorder. It is the worst place because a clinician sees the patient for only a brief period of time, and outside the context of his or her everyday world. But it is the best place, too, because the patient comes to the ER in some kind of crisis—real, imagined, or concocted—that intensely focuses issues in a way that favors uncovering the basic truth about a life.

I am often surprised by how much patients reveal about themselves during an ER evaluation, and how much of what they tell me does not support either their current psychiatric diagnosis or their claim for the service requested. Old hospital records, reports from others who come to the ER with the patient, and reports from those contacted by phone often fill out the patient's story, allowing the true clinical picture to unfold.

Kia's schizophrenia diagnosis was no doubt largely based on her report of auditory hallucinations. To me, the voices she claimed to hear were suspect. When I pressed her further about what she was hearing, nothing she said convinced me she had the perceptual distortions that fall under the rubric of auditory hallucinations. That she heard voices only when she ruminated about being raped made me think that, if these voices were auditory hallucinations (which I doubted), they were being driven by major depression, most likely fed by an Axis II disorder. Was her conscience "speaking" to her? Did she feel she had some complicity in her sexual abuse? Was her guilt "talking"?

Kia, 22, was brought to the ER by the police on emergency petition signed by a psychiatrist with whom she had just started working at a nearby community mental health center. The paperwork from this facility included an Application for Voluntary Admission to our psychiatry unit signed by Kia and her psychiatrist. The emergency petition stated that the patient was two-and-a-half-months pregnant and for the last two days had reported hearing voices instructing her to kill herself and her baby.

Kia was first hospitalized at age 13. She had been hospitalized 10 times since then, but not during the last year. Her outpatient psychiatric care had been sporadic. The current diagnosis was schizophrenia, but she had also been diagnosed with bipolar disorder. She had been taking Zyprexa and Prozac, but stopped taking these medications two months before because she thought she was pregnant. Kia did not smoke cigarettes and had never had legal problems. "I'm a good girl, up to a point," she told me. She denied ever using street drugs or abusing alcohol. "I'm scared to use drugs," she said sheepishly, as if this abstinence indicated some kind of weakness. Her toxicology screen was negative.

Unexpectedly, her urine pregnancy test was negative too. Confronted with this fact, Kia insisted she had had 18 unprotected sexual encounters during the last few months and volunteered that her period was about two weeks late. Never married, she was childless, though she had had two miscarriages. "I want to get pregnant," she told me convincingly. "I'm the only one in my family with no kids." Clearly, Kia felt disadvantaged by her barrenness. The current crisis began when her mother reacted negatively to the news—incorrect, as it turned out—that Kia was pregnant. Kia expected to be held in high esteem but was instead ridiculed.

Though she had finished one year at a community college, Kia had no job and was living with her mother. She was on welfare and received medical assistance. She had recently started a course in hairstyling but had stopped going to classes.

Shortly before the interview, I noticed Kia standing outside the room assigned to her. She was speaking amiably with another patient. As soon as I introduced myself, she was ready to talk and seemed eager for the evaluation to proceed. Kia was alert, focused, and cooperative.

She spoke easily and un–self-consciously. She gave the exact date without hesitation. Memory, recent and distant, was intact. Kia appeared moderately depressed and reported a decrease in appetite and sleep during the last few days. She seemed more needy than suicidal and denied having a plan to harm herself. There were small, well-healed cut marks on both wrists. Several years earlier, she had taken an overdose of 40 Tylenol tablets and had immediately gone to the ER. That was her only serious effort to harm herself.

In response to the standard interview question about sexual abuse, Kia replied that she had been raped at age 13 and added, "I don't want to talk about it." (Her first hospitalization was immediately after the rape.) Wondering if unresolved feelings associated with the sexual assault nine years earlier might be contributing to her present crisis, I tried to get some sense of what effort she had made to deal with this trauma; little, it turned out, either as an outpatient or during her 11 hospitalizations. Kia told me she did not want to talk to a man about being raped. I suggested that, if she were able to do so, she would overcome a significant hurdle in the therapeutic challenge to this trauma—her tendency to distrust and reject every member of the gender who had caused her pain. My words must have struck a chord because Kia, who until now had good control of herself and was engaging in a highly interactive dialogue, broke into heavy, heaving sobs. Putting her head down into her lap and hiding her face from me, she turned inward to the pain she apparently had avoided for so long. For several minutes, I said no more than a word here and there. I did not want to interfere with the contact she seemed to be making with parts of her experience that most likely had been long walled off.

Kia said very little from that point on, but what she did say cut like glass. She did not volunteer details about the rape. She alluded to later sexual encounters she considered demeaning, though not forced. A strong element of guilt and self-reprisal was obvious in her words. "I want my virginity and innocence back," she said, still sobbing. "I know I can't have that. It's gone. I have no respect for myself." I asked Kia if she had ever before gone so deeply into the painful feelings she was experiencing now. She said she had not. I wondered how much working-through might be occurring—how much she could let go of the defenses she had put up to deny and fend off the pain she had felt when she was raped. I wondered if this experience would be transformative, if she would now be able to live more of her life outside the emotional jail her rapist had put her in nine years before and from which she had done little to extricate herself.

Noting her affect, a Freudian-oriented observer would hope that Kia was abreacting the trauma by relinquishing defenses she had been using to avoid dealing with it. Someone more existentially oriented would see the outpouring of emotion as an unmasking of the self-deception behind Kia's denial of her possibilities for going beyond the trauma and perhaps even behind her unwillingness to face her own complicity in later consensual sexual acts, which she now felt were degrading. To a degree, Kia was also wallowing in self-pity.

Because Kia was currently diagnosed with schizophrenia, I looked carefully for symptoms of psychotic decompensation. Through her deep sobs, her speech, little as there was, stayed rational and goal-directed. There was no indication of formal thought disorder. She did not become paranoid or show any resentment toward me, despite my having helped to bring her in touch with this great pain. In fact, she seemed unburdened, relieved, and grateful. She did not report a return of the commanding voices she claimed to have heard earlier that day. I saw no striking sign of borderline dynamics or any indication of dissociation. Clearly, Kia had considerable ego strength, even under the kind of intense emotional pressure that often leads to decompensation.

I questioned her carefully about the voices she claimed had been telling her to harm herself and her (wished for, imagined, nonexistent) baby. The voices, she said, started when she was 13, after she was raped. The Zyprexa, which she had stopped taking two months earlier, when she started hoping and believing she might be pregnant, had done nothing to lessen these voices, which were periodic, not constant. "When I get stressed out, I hear voices," she told me. A few sentences later she narrowed her claim to, "I only hear voices when I think about the rape." Kia did not have the "feel" of someone with a schizophrenia spectrum disorder. She had none of the subtle oddness or bizarreness shown by most of the schizophrenics I have worked with. Nor was there any sign of the primary negative symptoms seen so often in patients with this illness. It seemed more likely to me that her withdrawal from life was due to a paralysis caused by her sexually induced trauma.

Kia's schizophrenia diagnosis was no doubt largely based on her report of auditory hallucinations. To me, the voices she claimed to hear were suspect. When I pressed her further about what she was hearing, nothing she said convinced me she had the perceptual distortions that fall under the rubric of auditory hallucinations. That she heard voices only when she ruminated about being raped made me think that, if these voices were auditory hallucinations (which I doubted), they were being driven by major depression, most likely fed by an Axis II disorder. Was her conscience "speaking" to her? Did she feel she had some complicity in her sexual abuse? Was her guilt "talking"?

Many patients who do not hear voices claim to hear them. Some do so to get attention, others to talk their way into a psychiatric bed or a disability check, or to get a lesser punishment for a crime. And some psychiatrists—lacking the clinical skill or the courage to challenge patients' assertions of auditory hallucinations, or wanting to help patients obtain disability so they can better fight their mental illness, or being just plain scared of getting sued for missing an Axis I diagnosis—accept the claim at face value. This acceptance can then strongly reinforce a patient's self-deceiving belief in, and claim to, a fictitious symptom and an incorrect diagnosis. Could this kind of reinforcement retrospectively create false memories of such perceptual experiences? And could these false memories then become the basis for further claims to having had these experiences? It is not hard to see how patients—particularly those with egos weakened and distorted by personality disorders or those with strong tendencies to dissociate—could come to *believe* they are hearing voices after even subtle encouragement by an authoritative mental health clinician.

When new patients arrive with a diagnosis of schizophrenia or bipolar disorder, many clinicians are reluctant to reverse the diagnosis, regardless of their doubts about its validity. Uncertainty about their diagnostic skills and fear of being sued if patients were to harm themselves or others after being taken off a neuroleptic, atypical antipsychotic, or mood-stabilizing medication are major reasons for this hesitancy. I often see patients in the ER, particularly those with substance-abuse and Axis II disorders, with diagnoses of schizophrenia spectrum and bipolar disorders, who *know* they do not have these illnesses. Sometimes, this is why they stop taking the neuroleptics, atypical antipsychotics, or mood stabilizers they were prescribed. When I ask how they got their diagnoses, a common response is, "That's what the doctor told me."

And that was Kia's answer when I asked why she felt she might have either schizophrenia or bipolar disorder. Trying to establish a clinical basis for her past bipolar diagnosis, I questioned her closely about the symptoms of a manic episode—the *DSM-IV* requires that a patient have at least one manic episode for a diagnosis of bipolar disorder. Kia had never had a distinct period of abnormally elevated, expansive, or irritable mood lasting at least one week. During that week (which never happened), she was not grandiose; nor did she need less sleep or talk more than usual; nor did she feel that her thoughts were racing or that she was distracted to the point where she could not function normally. She had no increase in goal-directed activity, nor did she excessively pursue pleasurable activities with a high potential for bad consequences. In spite of not meeting the *DSM-IV* criteria for bipolar disorder, Kia was given this diagnosis, allowing at least one clinician to avoid the hard work of dealing therapeutically with defenses that had all but crippled her life for nine years—all in the name of a chemical imbalance that could be treated only with medication.

Kia spent five days in the psychiatric unit. A second pregnancy test was also negative. Tests for genital herpes and chlamydia, diagnosed previously, were positive. One might wonder if Kia's failure to get pregnant was related to tubal damage from venereal disease and if her guilt over her sterility derived partially from this possibility. Did she feel that her body had been compromised and revictimized by her voluntary sexual activity? (The personal belongings checklist from her hospital chart listed only two items: keys and condoms. The latter seems strange for someone trying so hard to get pregnant.) And would such feelings make it harder for her to come to terms with her sexual violation at age 13?

Kia did not react well to the news that her second pregnancy test was negative. On her third hospital day, she told the staff she wanted to die because she was being "punished by God." Nursing notes record that she was loud, agitated, and threatening and that she threw furniture in her room. She was sedated with Haldol and Inapsine and spent at least one day in the seclusion room. One chart note stated, "Kia seizes opportunities to get attention"; another labeled her "a major attention getter." The day after admission, Kia produced this letter, neatly written on yellow, lined paper:

> I hate myself because I can't make babies! I cannot become pregnant because I'm not fertile. No one loves me or cares about me and if they do I would only push them away. I do not want to live at all. I need the pain in my heart to decline out of existence along with me. My heart cries and no one including me can wipe them [the tears] away! The only one who could is God, but I hate him because he is punishing me. First with my rapes and now he won't give me what I want most, a baby. He just don't want me to be happy. I hate God! I hate myself! I hate everybody! I need to die A.S.A.P! I have a goal to achieve and that's kill myself last [a happy face is drawn here] then take a hanger and put it in my vagina and pull with all my might! A instant, do it yourself removal of my uterus, womb, ovaries and fallopian tubes. Why not! Anyway what do you do with something useless; you dispose of it! Why should I strive to live when I deserve to die?

Eight exclamation points! Through the bathos, Kia lets us know what her life is up to. She is angry at herself, the world, and God. She blames her sterility alternately on the rape (curiously, we hear no criticism of the rapist), herself, and God. She allows no forgiveness for any of the parties involved, and there is no transcendence. She is stuck in her pain and converts old pain into new pain daily, so that every day is a new crucifixion. Kia lives in a cocoon spun from anger and resentment. Her victimization is reinforced at every turn by a society that prizes the victim, but offers Kia no reward for this condition beyond confirming her identity as a victim. And how does she reward herself? With the perverse satisfaction of her own negative feelings, the feelings that go with being a victim. How "comforting" and "satisfying" that anger must be.

Every sentence Kia writes puts her center stage. She is the main character in a drama she sees as having no satisfactory outcome. She imagines being violent toward the body that betrayed her by becoming sterile. She will punish the organs that will not give her a child. Kia lives in the middle of this hysterical soap opera, this play-act of her life. There was another, briefer letter in her chart, this one addressed directly to God:

God please forgive my sins. Please take me away from here or I will do it myself. Lord yes I want to run away because I have no purpose here. No one wants to feel hurt and anger all their life. These intense internal feelings are killing me so I want to take the final step. I want eternal silence and forever departure so please, please kill me.

The letter is signed, "Forever in your name. Amen." A circle face is drawn below the closing: the mouth is turned down, and three teardrops fall from the left eye. Kia's threats of self-harm seem more like a self-pitying self-dramatization of her situation than the formulation of a death scenario. Neither letter reveals a hint of psychosis. Kia's pathology seems mostly Axis II, of the histrionic type, possibly with some component of posttraumatic stress.

After our interview, while waiting in my office to be escorted to the psychiatric unit, Kia became eerily quiet, coquettish, and childlike. It occurred to me that she was acknowledging her inability to process the feelings she had just experienced about her sexual trauma and was appealing to me to rescue her from these feelings. This is classic histrionic pathology. According to the *DSM-IV,* "the essential feature of Histrionic Personality Disorder is pervasive and excessive emotionality and attention-seeking behavior."

The attending psychiatrist who took care of Kia while she was in the hospital agreed that the schizophrenia diagnosis appeared untenable. He decided to continue the Zyprexa temporarily (not as an antipsychotic, but for the capacity of this medication to act as a tranquilizing "ego glue") and added Depakote, also temporarily, hoping it would stabilize her mood. Prozac was discontinued. Neither Zyprexa nor Depakote, separately or together, would fix what was wrong with Kia. They could only calm her down and limit the emotional and somatic consequences of the pathological dynamics of her histrionic personality. Kia's only hope of ridding herself of her core illness is to work intensely with a therapist who knows how to challenge the defenses that make her a victim (and make her special in her own mind) and to challenge what keeps her on stage and out of the instrumental world—the only venue where nonpathological life can be attempted.

Patients are damaged by being told they have a mental disorder when they show neither the behavior nor the dynamics specified by the current standard for psychiatric diagnosis. (The *DSM-IV* is the current standard, but many nosologically inclined clinicians have honestly tried to define what psychopathology is, and their diagnostic schema deserve consideration as well.) A false diagnosis often leads ineluctably to prescribing the wrong medication: a neuroleptic or one of the newer atypical antipsychotics, when a minor tranquilizer would be adequate to manage symptoms and would cause fewer side effects; a mood stabilizer, when an antidepressant would do; or an antidepressant before a therapeutic alliance has been attempted and time for working through has been allowed. A false diagnosis also keeps patient and therapist from confronting the defenses constituting the actual mental disorder and may even induce patients to think, feel, and behave as if they have the pathology falsely attributed to them by a bogus diagnostic tag.

I saw Kia again in the ER six months later. Her chief complaints at that time were abdominal pain and depression. She had stopped taking her lithium, Prozac, and Risperdal two weeks before, after being switched from Zyprexa and Depakote by her psychiatrist at the community mental health center where she was followed. Kia told me that a friend owned a gun and that she would get the gun from her and use it on herself. She was clearly upset and depressed and wanted to be admitted to the psychiatric unit.

Asked if she was hearing voices, Kia said the last voice she heard was two years before—it had called her a whore and told her no one loved her. My guess is that some family member, probably her mother, had addressed these words to Kia after she reported one of her numerous sexual encounters and that the put-down stuck. Kia's statement that she had not heard voices for two years undercut her claim in the interview six months earlier that voices at the time were telling her to kill herself and her (nonexistent) baby.

Kia was hospitalized and had a rocky five-day stay in the psychiatric unit. She was irritable and verbally abusive and required sedation and seclusion. She repeatedly denied hearing voices or having any thoughts of self-harm. The threat made in the ER to shoot herself, which I never took literally, quickly disappeared. There was no mention of mania or hypomania in the chart. The diagnosis was major depression, recurrent, severe, without psychotic features. Kia told the staff that her pelvic pain had started after a recent sexual encounter.

Not long after I saw Kia in the ER the second time, it occurred to me that her clinical picture was consistent with a pathological personality type that Donald F. Klein calls *hysteroid dysphoria*—"a chronic nonpsychotic disturbance involving repeated episodes of abruptly depressed mood in response to feeling rejected." Many of Kia's worst episodes of depression and behavioral dyscontrol followed sexual encounters, some of which she insisted were rapes. Kia has made it clear that, for her, any sexual act is ridden with guilt. Does she feel retraumatized and revictimized because of her rape at age 13? Is sex for Kia ultimately an act of rejection—of her desired, virginal, non-violated self?

Klein describes hysteroid dysphoric patients this way:

> Their normal state is characterized by behavior that is ebullient, histrionic, flamboyant, intrusive, seductive, self-centered or demanding. Normal mood is often expansive and active. Applause is highly stimulating and rewarding. Poor social judgment is specifically reflected by inappropriate love objects that are quickly over-idealized. Suicidal threats and gestures are common during depressive episodes as are social withdrawal and self-mutilative acts such as scratching, burning or picking of skin. Completed suicide is rare.

That is a rather good portrait of Kia. Perhaps it was her "expansive" mood that was mistaken for mania, and that may be how she got the bipolar diagnosis.

What is to be done for Kia? First, she needs to start dealing with the trauma of her sexual abuse and her mostly histrionic defense against it, which have led to the devastation that is her life. At the same time, she needs to be supported with medications that control her symptoms, which are primarily depression, anxiety, and agitation. This is what her psychiatrist and the treatment team at the community mental health center where she is followed have been trying to do. The course has been rough, since Kia has been unwilling to follow the program set up for her. She is demanding, does only what she wants to do, and plays one staff member off against another.

Kia continues to feel, think, and behave in ways more like someone with a personality disorder (histrionic) than someone with a biologically driven chemical imbalance (bipolar disorder). She hews more to Axis II than to Axis I, to the degree that this distinction has clinical validity in her case. Klein's notion of hysteroid dysphoria nicely undercuts this dubious dichotomy, conflating the psychopathologies of personality structure and mood.

None of this is to deny that Kia's early sexual trauma may have been imprinted somehow in the neural circuitry of her brain, impairing (though not fully negating) her freedom to think, feel, and behave in a more normal way and inclining her toward Axis II. Not to be denied either is the possibility that over time, in response to adequate psychotherapy and positive life experience, some of Kia's aberrant neural circuitry can be "rewired," leading to a less pathological neural substrate and a less pathological life.

Part III

Veiled and Bizarre Stories

These stories show how some patients use the emergency room to advance their psychopathological projects and how the ER may become a setting for bizarre events.

The ER is often the last resort for some people who do not know how to live their lives, even at the most basic level, and want to be taken care of. These patients make up stories about why they should be given a bed in a psychiatric unit. Many feign psychiatric symptoms, particularly auditory hallucinations ("I'm hearing voices telling me to kill myself"), or they claim, often untruthfully, to be suicidal or homicidal. Some patients, when their bluff is called and they are told they will be discharged, become angry and verbally abusive. Many unmasked patients head straight for another ER to try the same con, or maybe a different one.

The chart from Stan's last admission to our psychiatric unit included this comment by the psychiatrist who was following him as an outpatient: "The patient will show up at an ER, claim to be a 'rapid cycler'—either hypomanic or depressed—that he is suicidal, that he needs to be hospitalized. If not admitted, he will go to another hospital with the same story. I have never known him to make a suicide attempt."

The *DSM-IV* does not consider "malingering" a diagnosis but designates this behavior as a V Code. V codes are assigned to a number of conditions when it is not clear that a maladaptive behavior is due to a mental disorder, though the dysfunction is often significant enough to require some clinical intervention.

Most ER malingerers are patients who have Axis I or Axis II disorders. These disorders may, in a sense, predispose a patient to malinger and manipulate, but this behavior is not a direct manifestation of the disorder, as, for example, an auditory hallucination is a manifestation of the neural derangement that almost certainly underlies schizophrenia. The *DSM-IV* defines malingering as "the intentional production of false or grossly exaggerated physical or psychological symptoms, motivated by external incentives." I have selected three of the most egregious malingerers from the many I saw in the ER. These choices were based on the outrageousness of what these patients requested, as well as on how often they came to the ER asking for it.

Lucy, 44, was diagnosed with paranoid schizophrenia. She was morbidly obese, with her excess weight distributed in various rounded protrusions from her midsection, buttocks, and thighs. Her walk was lumbering, and her speech was all in the lower register—slow, drawling, and suggesting low intelligence (she had gone through the 10th grade in special education classes). Lucy was followed by a team affiliated with a university hospital. Members of this team helped her find an apartment and manage her money. Lucy was chronically dissatisfied with what these capable and caring clinicians were doing for her. In fact, that is why she kept coming to the ER. Sometimes by exhortations, sometimes by threats, Lucy tried to get us to intervene on her behalf so she could get what she wanted: a better apartment, more money, a chance to move to another part of the state to be near her relatives (who did not want her with them).

A member of the team that followed Lucy was on 24-hour call, and Lucy would think nothing of asking the ER staff to contact that person at any hour, day or night. During an interview that began at 5:30 a.m., Lucy's first words to me were, "Please call the team and tell them to treat me a little better. They don't smile and shake my hand anymore." She was dead serious. I called, and was told that Lucy had a habit of going to ERs all over the city with the same complaints and demands.

Lucy's paranoid schizophrenia seemed under good control. Though she constantly complained, her complaints had the flavor of bitchiness and ingratitude, not paranoia. On the four occasions when I interviewed her, she denied auditory or visual hallucinations and delusions and showed no sign of formal thought disorder. In no sense could she be said to be in relapse. On the other hand, the course of her schizophrenia was chronic, she had significant negative symptoms, and her behavior was disorganized. None of these facets of her illness explained her malingering and manipulation. Perhaps one could say that she chose to act this way but made the choice with a compromised biological and psychological substrate.

Lucy's most recent hospitalization had been more than a year earlier. She was compliant with her psychiatric medication: Haldol, Cogentin, and Klonopin. She also took Glucotrol for Type 2 diabetes mellitus. Lucy was HIV-positive but did not have AIDS. She said she had contracted the virus "from sex." The last time Lucy came to the ER I told her that I would not evaluate her and that she needed to take her complaints directly to the clinical team who was following her. She wanted to change providers and be seen by the outpatient service at our hospital. I gave her the number to call for an intake evaluation. But I felt it was unlikely that Lucy would be satisfied with anything any provider did for her.

The second patient who stands out as an exemplary malingerer and manipulator is Stan, 43, a college graduate. In 1977, shortly after his wife had left him, Stan turned his car westward for an extended road trip, without telling anyone anything about his destination (perhaps he had none at the time). His parents hired a private detective, who eventually tracked him down at a motel in Las Vegas. He was brought back to this city, hospitalized, and diagnosed with manic-depressive illness.

To get some sense of just how "bipolar" Stan was, I asked what symptoms of elevated mood he had had during his trip. He acknowledged some expansiveness of self-concept but denied having periods of unusual productivity or being able to go for several days without sleep. He did feel he had spent more money than he should have spent, but "not more money than [he] had." Stan did not use drugs or alcohol at that time, or any time after. There were no other "manic" episodes after 1977.

Stan insisted that he was a "rapid cycler," his mood shifting from hypomania to depression in cycles lasting days or weeks. He was taking lithium, Depakote, and Risperdal, as well as Synthroid. Stan claimed that he became depressed the day before and suicidal just hours prior to coming to the ER. "I am in the same shape I was in when I was admitted to this hospital a few months ago," he explained. His admission had been two months earlier and was the most recent of nearly 40 admissions (two a year, he said) since 1977. Asked what he was thinking of doing to hurt himself, he responded, "Cutting myself with sharps." He explained that he would use a "shard of glass" to cut his wrist. He showed me one wrist with a barely visible old scar, as if to demonstrate his commitment to this plan. "I tried to cut my wrist several years ago," he explained.

Stan neither looked nor sounded depressed. Sleep and appetite were undisturbed. He was reading a Joseph Wambaugh novel as I entered the room to begin the interview. He greeted me pleasantly and smiled and joked appropriately throughout the interview. I asked what had led up to his feeling depressed and suicidal. He ticked off the following reasons: he had a sinus infection; he was looking for a job; he was not getting along with the other members of the group home where he was living; and, just the day before, his brother had refused to give him money to move. Clearly, Stan wanted to be admitted to the psychiatric unit. I asked him several times what he would do if he was not admitted. Cutting his wrist and going to another hospital were the alternatives he was considering.

At this point, it was necessary to contact someone who knew the patient and his baseline behavior. I called the care provider at the group home where Stan had lived for two years. He said that Stan went to the ER every time he had a problem. He added that he had never known Stan to make an attempt to hurt himself. I called a hospital staff psychiatrist who had worked with Stan during one of his admissions to the psychiatric unit. "What you have to understand about him," the psychiatrist said, "is that he is very manipulative." The chart from Stan's last admission to our psychiatric unit included this comment by the psychiatrist who was following him as an outpatient: "The patient will show up at an ER, claim to be a 'rapid cycler'—either hypomanic or depressed—that he is suicidal, that he needs to be hospitalized. If not admitted, he will go to another hospital with the same story. I have never known him to make a suicide attempt."

Stan, it seems, was up to his old tricks. Told he would be discharged from the ER, he followed through on his game plan and proudly announced that he would go to another hospital and try for admission there. Reading between the lines of his story, it seemed his main objective now was to manipulate his brother into giving him the money to move out of the group home, where he was unhappy, and into accommodations more to his liking.

Stan's "rapid cycling" may have been nothing more than the intense emotional roller coaster that so many people with borderline personality disorder and histrionic personality disorder ride. It is also possible that Stan's malingering, which included the fabrication and amplification of some symptoms, derived in part from his having significant dependent personality disorder traits. For some patients, facing life with the mask of a serious, chronic mental disorder such as bipolar disorder is preferred to facing it straight on.

Though Lucy and Stan occupy secure places in my pantheon of ER malingerers and manipulators, the single most memorable ploy came from another patient, Ricky. Ricky, 28, told us that he had been brought to the ER by his sister, who was visiting from out of town and had walked in on him as he was about "to eat [his] brother's loaded gun." And what had caused Ricky to be in such a desperate state? This was his story: Ricky, his mother, his twin brother, and his sister had driven to Atlanta for his grandmother's funeral. Just before leaving Atlanta to return home, Ricky had a fight with his mother and decided to come back on his own. While en route, the van, driven by his brother, crashed, and everyone was killed. Ricky's lamentations included, "If only I didn't have that fight with my mother . . ." and "If I had been driving, I would not have fallen asleep at the wheel"— which was what his brother had done, he claimed.

Ricky told me he was angry at God for allowing this tragedy to happen. He did not see how he could go on with his life. "Do you know how hard it is to lose a twin brother?" he asked (so convincingly that I had to acknowledge to myself that I did not). "We shared everything," he wanted me to understand. To hear him tell it, he was overwhelmed with grief and guilt. Ricky told me he was considering several ways of ending his life. He wanted to be hospitalized, presumably to spare himself from the consequences of his destructive impulses.

Ricky admitted to heavily using alcohol and cocaine since he was a teenager, but he never had any treatment for substance abuse (his toxicology screen was positive for cocaine and negative for alcohol). Four years earlier, he had been diagnosed with bipolar disorder. He was hospitalized at that time and a second time two years later. (I suspect that this diagnosis was not warranted by the clinical facts, as happens so often with those who abuse drugs.) Ricky was getting disability payments for his "bipolar disorder." Asked if he did any work, he replied, "I'm a backyard mechanic."

Ricky also claimed to have a seizure disorder and to have taken Neurontin, Tegretol, Zoloft, and Zyprexa until a week before he came to the ER, when he "ran out" of these medications. "The only medicine I'm taking now is Viagra," he told me, as if he believed that was the only pill he needed. When I reminded him that this drug could be fatal if mixed with certain other drugs, he replied, "You have just given me an idea for how to kill myself."

The story Ricky was telling seemed far-fetched, but it also had some face validity. He kept things low-key and never demanded to be hospitalized, as so many malingering patients do. "The only reason I came to the ER was for my sister," he wanted me to believe. This sister, who, he said, had taken the gun he was about to "eat" to the police station, was nowhere to be found. Supposedly, she lived an hour away and immediately after dropping Ricky off at the ER had driven home to take care of her children—no one in the ER had seen or spoken to her. Ricky claimed not to know her phone number or her address. Nor did he know the phone numbers of any other of his surviving siblings. "They're all drug addicts," he told me, as if this meant there was no way I could expect to contact them. When I called the number he claimed was for his mother's house—where he had allegedly been staying since the accident and where allegedly his sister had gone earlier that day to see about "settling the estate" and ended up serendipitously foiling his suicide attempt—a recorded message said that the line had been disconnected. Ricky insisted the phone had worked earlier that day. "The phone company must have just disconnected it," was his surprised response. Hearing this, his nurse said she was pretty sure phone service would not be cut off on a Saturday!

As hard as we tried, there was no way to check Ricky's story. He assured me that he could return to his deceased mother's house, which he claimed was now partly his. The ER attending and the nurse who worked with him both felt this story was, in effect, too good to be true. So did I, but I suppose that was my night "to err on the side of caution," and I had him admitted to the psychiatric unit in a nearby hospital. Two days later, I called the psychiatrist who was working with him. "This is the second time Ricky's family has been wiped out in a car accident," she said. "He got the story from a local newspaper." Which meant this was the second time this "disaster" had bought him a psychiatric bed as an antidote to homelessness brought on, no doubt, by his long-time drug abuse. I told the psychiatrist that I felt Ricky had put on an Academy Award performance. But all performances must end, and she related how the curtain had fallen on this one. "Ricky had trouble keeping his story straight. Yesterday, he called his mother from the unit. I'm discharging him today. The only medication he wanted from me was Viagra." He didn't get it.

We have been stiffed by patients before, but this one still hurts.

While I was working as a research associate in the Department of Psychiatry at the University of Maryland, this bit of clinical wisdom found its way to me: "There are few real emergencies in psychiatry." It took several years of evaluating psychiatric patients in the ER for the full significance of these words to hit home. The fact is that we who work in the ER spend most of our time dealing with unspectacular, though not necessarily uninteresting, cases. To get a better hold on what we see, it is useful to create categories for certain kinds of stories that we hear over and over. The frequently seen "dump" is one well-known category. A dump occurs when someone responsible for the care of another person is no longer able—or willing—to bear the responsibility and brings that person to the ER. Clinicians of all kinds, parents of young children, children of aged parents, staff of nursing homes, and the police do most of this dumping.

It had taken three hours to get to the bottom of this case and to finesse the situation so that Marsha felt as if she were getting enough from us to render her manipulation no longer worthwhile.

This first story illustrates how a dump can draw the ER into an agenda that does not put the patient's best interests first. Roger, 38, was diagnosed with bipolar disorder at age 19. He had been hospitalized about 20 times but was stable for the last four or five years. He was being seen weekly by a psychiatrist and a therapist. His medications were Trilafon and Pamelor, which he took as prescribed.

Roger came to the ER on emergency petition taken out by his mother. Decreased sleep, increased agitation, and threatening behavior were the reasons stipulated for the ER evaluation. Roger immediately took exception to what the petition claimed; he denied that he was causing the conflict at home that brought him to the ER. He was sleeping six to eight hours a night, as usual, had a good appetite, and had not lost weight. He looked serious and concerned but denied feeling depressed, though he did acknowledge feeling "strange." He could describe previous manic episodes that had required hospitalization, but he had no current manic symptoms, including the grandiosity—"thinking I'm someone important"—that marked earlier relapses. He had no plan to hurt himself or anyone else.

Roger's speech was articulate, had a normal volume and rate, and was goal directed. His insight was good: he seemed to understand the nature of his chronic mental illness and was making a convincing case against the specifics of the emergency petition. His judgment was good: he was compliant with treatment and took an active part in the ER evaluation. The toxicology screen was negative for alcohol and drugs of abuse.

Roger had lived with his mother for the last six years. She insisted on his living with her so that his disability check could be used to help pay the mortgage. The mother had recently remarried, and, when her other son moved in, the expanded household spawned new conflicts. When Roger proposed moving out, emotions rose, triggering the 911 call and the emergency petition. In spite of what was going on at home, the young man wanted to return there. I was unable to contact the mother by phone, and it occurred to me that she was deliberately making herself unavailable. I did reach Roger's psychiatrist and his therapist. Both had seen him recently, and neither noticed any sign of relapse. I discharged the patient with the recommendation that he talk with these clinicians about finding a new place to live. Following the money here may be the key to understanding this dump.

The ER is also dumped on by the police. Some people who are arrested have made threats and gestures of self-harm and are then brought to us for evaluation. Usually, their motives are transparent, and they can be discharged back to their jailers. One of the most memorable of these cases was a 17-year-old girl who was taken into custody after she had been found soliciting on a highway that was a notorious venue for prostitution and drug dealing. The police brought her to the ER when she told them she had a plan to kill herself.

Marsha had been evaluated earlier that day by a social worker with the crisis team at the hospital. Judged not to be a threat to herself or others, she was released back to police custody. While in the lockup the second time, Marsha tied her brassiere around her neck in the presence of a police officer and told him she was planning to hang herself with this undergarment. Because of her threat, she was brought back to the ER for a second evaluation and placed in seclusion.

My interview with this patient began at 2:30 a.m. Immediately, I sensed her anger, which substance abusers often show when called to task for the consequences of their addiction. Marsha spoke in short bursts, giving only brief answers to some questions, altogether refusing to answer other questions. She was particularly resentful about being interviewed twice in one day and took a combative stance toward me. She refused to discuss the specifics of her mood but did deny ever having had auditory or visual hallucinations. Nothing in her speech or demeanor suggested any psychotic process.

Marsha acknowledged having smoked four dime bags of cocaine that day and stated that she had been using this drug for several years. She had had one admission to a psychiatric hospital four years earlier but refused to specify the reason. Currently, she had no outpatient psychiatric treatment. "I prostitute myself to support my coke habit," she eventually told me, with no detectable sign of embarrassment or regret. "I want to kill myself because I have nothing to live for." For almost two hours, Marsha stuck doggedly to her claim that she wanted to end her life. She stated that, if she had to go back to jail, she would hang herself with her brassiere. To me, this threat was palpably absurd. But, her threat having been made loudly to the police, we could not discharge her. They had dutifully stayed in the ER for several hours, then returned to district headquarters when the case became stalemated.

After the arrest, the police had contacted Marsha's mother. She refused to come to the station to sign out her daughter, a minor. I felt certain that, stuck with the choice of doing time in jail or spending several days in a psychiatric facility, this patient would say what she knew she needed to say to avoid jail. I called her mother. She told me that the girl had never done anything to hurt herself but often made threats to do so when she was in stressful situations—like this one, no doubt.

I asked the mother if she would be willing to appear at her daughter's hearing later that day, if Marsha promised to get treatment for her co-caine addiction (though I had no reason to believe that this addict was ready to make any major changes in her life). I was surprised when the mother immediately agreed to do this. I have often talked with parents, relatives, and the significant others of drug and alcohol abusers in the ER who had been betrayed once too often and refused to do anything more for the person who had betrayed them. When I relayed the mother's offer of help, Marsha immediately accepted it and dropped the threat to harm herself.

I finished my report at 5:30 a.m. It had taken three hours to get to the bottom of this case and to finesse the situation so that Marsha felt as if she were getting enough from us to render her manipulation no longer worthwhile. The police returned, and took her back to jail. Twice in one day she had maneuvered them into dumping her on us (the police just followed the rules, doing what they had to do). At least we had not been manipulated into giving her a psychiatric bed. We might have been, had the mother not agreed to help.

Families and the police are not the only ones who dump mentally ill patients on the ER; doctors do this as well. Sharon, a woman in her mid-30s, was brought in by the police on emergency petition taken out by her psychiatrist. Sharon had repeatedly called the psychiatrist at home for several days, ignoring requests that she stop. In the ER, she was agitated and angry about having been removed from her apartment by the police. There was no indication that she was suicidal or wanted to harm (as opposed to annoy) her doctor. Sharon vociferously insisted that she did not need hospitalization and demanded to go home, threatening to sue us if we did not discharge her.

I called the psychiatrist, who told me that this patient had been harassing her and insisted that she be hospitalized. In fact, the psychiatrist was tired of being bothered and wanted to teach her tormentor a lesson. This obviously borderline patient was going through a rough patch and was dragging her doctor along for the ride, as borderline patients often do. My choices were to commit Sharon to a psychiatric unit or cut her loose. Taking her freedom away to spare the psychiatrist further annoyance did not seem justified. I empathized with the psychiatrist but advocated for the patient, and sent Sharon home. I could only hope that she would be "scared straight" by her brush with an unwanted psychiatric admission.

Another kind of ER story worthy of a category is the "stumble." This metaphor captures something essential about the way many of our patients come to us. A stumble occurs when someone with a chronic mental illness acts in a disorganized or bizarre manner, becomes frightened, and then heads for the ER. The police, acting on their own or on a tip, facilitate many stumbles. Often, the threat is more imagined than real. Usually, these patients can be reassured, redirected, and discharged. Persons who are not mentally ill also find ways of stumbling into the ER. (As far as I know, the stumble category has not been designated before, and I would be honored if it were to become a part of ER lore.)

Off her medication for one month, and under the new stress of not finding her former boyfriend where she expected him to be, as well as being far from home with no money to return there, this schizophrenic patient probably experienced a brief, minor decompensation that rapidly cleared once she was reassured and catered to by the ER staff.

I think of this stumble of a 32-year-old woman as poignant. Barbara lived with her boyfriend and members of his family. This day, wanting to look up an old boyfriend she had not seen for a long time who lived some distance away, she walked to the house where she last knew him to live, only to be told that he had moved. Barbara was then too discouraged and too tired to walk home. "I called 911," she told me during the interview. "I was getting scared. I didn't have any money to get home." Barbara expected the police to drive her home. To ensure that she would be taken seriously, Barbara told the officer who responded that she felt suicidal. Instead of taking her home, the officer, after filling out an emergency petition, brought Barbara to the ER, probably the last place she expected to be that day.

Diagnosed with schizophrenia, the patient was regularly seeing a psychiatrist and a therapist at a community mental health center. She had been taking Haldol and Cogentin but stopped these medications a month earlier because, she claimed, they made her feel paranoid.

Barbara knew who she was, where she was, and the date. But she did seem spacey, sad, and childlike. She spoke slowly and paused noticeably before answering even the most basic questions. It seemed that every word required a major effort on her part. Asked to describe her mood, Barbara said she was depressed, but she denied disturbances of sleep and appetite, as well as weight loss. There were no auditory or visual hallucinations and no signs of formal thought disorder, and she was not feeling paranoid. Barbara categorically denied any intent or plan to harm herself or anyone else. She had never abused drugs or alcohol.

When I asked Barbara what she felt should happen next, she replied, "I want a ride home." (What she had put herself and us through to achieve this simple goal!) I told the physician assistant who had medically cleared her that I had no doubt she could be discharged. This normally placid and very competent woman looked at me as if I had lost my mind and asked, disbelievingly, "*What?*" During the physician assistant's interview, which was done at least an hour before mine, Barbara had acted bizarrely and had given little useful information. The physician assistant assumed that she was headed for a psychiatric bed. I suggested that she go back and talk to Barbara again. After the second interview, she agreed that the patient could go home.

Off her medication for one month, and under the new stress of not finding her former boyfriend where she expected him to be, as well as being far from home with no money to return there, this schizophrenic patient probably experienced a brief, minor decompensation that rapidly cleared once she was reassured and catered to by the ER staff. When I asked Barbara if she felt any different than she normally does, she replied, "I feel like the same person I was two or three weeks ago." (She was spending most of her time these days watching TV in the apartment she shared with her boyfriend and his family.) I called the boyfriend's father, and he agreed to take Barbara home.

This next stumble can only be described as heartbreaking. Andy, a 23-year-old male graduate student, was brought to the ER just after midnight by the police on emergency petition after he picked up a Baretta during an argument with his girlfriend and her ex-boyfriend. The other two principals in this event became alarmed and called 911. "I slid the barrel back to make sure it wasn't loaded," Andy told me. (It was not. I regret not asking why the gun happened to be at hand or why Andy picked it up at a moment of such high emotional acuity.)

The young man clearly was in a state of disbelief over having to explain how all this had happened. Andy's eyes were downcast, and he spoke through tears. Asked how he felt, he replied, with detachment and mordant understatement, "I'm not inordinately happy now." His sleep was good, but his appetite was off and he had lost about 10 pounds during the last two months. A year earlier, Andy had graduated from a prestigious university and was taking graduate courses in public health. School was going well, though he did admit to what he called "indecision." Clearly, he had symptoms of depression, but overall this seemed more like an adjustment disorder than major depression.

Andy had no psychiatric history, drank alcohol only occasionally and moderately, and denied using illicit drugs. He convinced me that, when he picked up the Baretta, he did not intend to harm himself or the two other persons involved in the argument. What Andy wanted now was to go home. "I just need to start getting my life back together," he told me in a way that made me think he wasn't only mouthing the words.

I suggested that Andy call his parents, who lived in another state, but he would not hear of it. He had no insurance, so I referred him to a community mental health center, where he could be seen at little or no cost. Since it was 4:30 a.m., I offered Andy a cab voucher, but he chose to walk back to his apartment building a few blocks away. I could only imagine what this solid citizen would feel as he entered the lobby of the building from which he had been led out in handcuffs by the police a few hours earlier—or what he was going to say to his girlfriend, who lived in the same building, once this night was over.

Dumps and stumbles are the bread and butter of what we do in the ER. Identifying patients who are being dumped, or who are stumbling in, allows me to connect their stories to similar stories I have already heard, processed, and learned from. Drawing from this experience, I have a better shot at giving these patients what they need, not more or less. Though not "real emergencies," dumps and stumbles can be occasions for real therapeutic encounter.

16　　　Murder and Mayhem, Maybe

Most of what the psychiatry service deals with in the ER could be classified as unnecessary visits, routine psychiatric emergencies (most of which are not actual emergencies), or real human tragedy. A fourth category could be called the bizarre. With a bizarre patient, the clinician often is not sure what is really going on and has no way of finding out. Confronted with a strange story that cannot be verified or disproved in the ER, and being asked to make a therapeutic response and a disposition, the clinician must face the limits of what psychiatry has to offer.

It seemed likely that someone, possibly the police, might be on his trail because of his assault the night before. Many people come to the ER to escape the consequences of their actions, and it occurred to me that Juan might have done that. But it made no sense for him to invent a murder just to get himself off the street.

Juan was sitting fully clothed on a gurney, his legs hanging over the side. It was a warm day in late September, and he had dressed accordingly. His shirt, sleeves rolled up, was open halfway down his chest. He wore shorts. Only his heavy boots seemed out of season.

Juan, 28, looked as though he had just come from the South Seas. A dark blue bandanna, with a white checkered pattern along the edges, was tied at the back of his head, covering his hair. Trinkets—a metal cross, a large key of the type used in colonial door locks, and several other objects—hung from a round cord circling his throat. Juan looked like a pirate. Sitting on the gurney, he carefully sketched what looked like a cross on a blank page of a bound notebook he had brought with him.

"I want to get some psychiatric help. I need some answers. Why do I feel this way?" These were Juan's first words to me. Then he told me this story. Eleven months earlier, a woman he was involved with made him a proposition: if Juan would kill a man who had been abusive to her, she would marry him. To Juan, it seemed a straightforward proposal. He shot the man and buried him in a rural area outside the city with the woman's help (the pirate had his buried treasure). From Juan's perspective, the only problem was that three days after he completed his end of the bargain, the woman who had proposed it deserted him.

Juan apparently had not been able to get over his girlfriend's betrayal. Four months earlier, he came to the ER for treatment of a serious, self-inflicted knife wound to his right forearm. He was admitted to a medical floor for one day. He intended to harm himself then, he said, but denied wanting to do so now. He insisted, however, that he would hurt anyone he knew to be sexually involved with his ex-girlfriend. He told me that the night before he had broken the legs of a man he was sure had had sex with her. He denied any intention or plan to harm the woman herself.

Juan had grown up in what he called "different parts" of the city. "I have no family," he told me. He finished the ninth grade and worked for a time in construction. Now and then, he did odd jobs. He was living nearby, in a working-class section of the city, but had not been to his room for several days. Juan acknowledged having been jailed 10 times for offenses that included assault and battery, breaking and entering, and violation of probation. He was currently on probation.

Juan's health was good, except for what he called a "slight problem with asthma." He took no medication. He denied any psychiatric history. (I do not know how he escaped psychiatric evaluation after stabbing himself in the arm and being treated for this injury in an ER.) He had been "speedballing" heroin and cocaine for about 10 years, using up to $60 worth of these substances a day. He acknowledged having used a small amount of heroin and cocaine the day before, but his toxicology screen was negative.

To hear Juan tell it, he knew no one in the city. With no family, friends, or psychiatric history, it was impossible to check his story. It seemed likely that someone, possibly the police, might be on his trail because of his assault the night before. Many people come to the ER to escape the consequences of their actions, and it occurred to me that Juan might have done that. But it made no sense for him to invent a murder just to get himself off the street.

Juan denied ever having had psychotic symptoms and showed no signs of psychosis during the interview. His flow of thought was normal, and his thought content was rational. Though I could not verify his bizarre story, I was inclined to believe it.

Juan seemed genuinely perplexed and troubled because, after keeping his part of the bargain, his then-girlfriend had not kept hers. "How could she do this?" he asked in wonderment. It seemed as if he could not grasp even the possibility of such a betrayal. That, he said, is why he came to the ER. "Psychologists and psychiatrists understand people," he said. "I came here to get help figuring this out."

It strains belief that someone capable of the evil to which Juan admitted could not understand how another person might betray him. (Is love that blind? Perhaps.) Maybe Juan was a sociopath and had no concept of evil, his or anyone else's. At no time during the interview did he show any sign of regret or remorse about killing one man and seriously assaulting another. The focus was solely on *his* pain.

After finishing the interview, I left the room to make several phone calls. When I returned, Juan was completing the drawing of the cross he had started earlier. The name of his ex-girlfriend was carefully printed on the horizontal beam. "RIH" was lettered on the vertical beam, above her name. He told me this meant "Rest in Hell." (I recalled that the usual notation here is RIP, or Rest in Peace.) The bottom of the cross had a sharp point, like a picket. Clearly, this was the drawing of a grave marker.

Juan could not be discharged from the ER. Considering what he told us he had already done, no one could predict what he would do next. The on-call psychiatrist was hesitant about accepting Juan for the inpatient unit. This was his "first murderer," as he put it, and mine as well. We talked about calling the police, but we wondered about the ethics of doing so. In spite of our doubts about what all this meant, Juan was allowed to sign himself into the unit. He insisted again that he wanted us to help him understand why, after he committed murder for a woman he obviously cared about, she did not return the favor by keeping her word to marry him. The psychiatrist did eventually contact the police. They were not able to verify the crimes Juan claimed to have committed.

Part IV

Stories with a Medical Component

These stories are about patients whose psychiatric symptoms were caused by physiological problems—a reminder that psychiatry has some of its roots in medicine.

17 Why Is This Schizophrenic Patient Hearing Voices?

Many patients who come to the ER are on multiple medications. It is not unusual to see three, four, five, or more psychiatric drugs listed in the nurse's note on the chart. Often, several other drugs are prescribed for medical problems such as asthma, hypertension, diabetes, and hypothyroidism. How can one hope to know the physiological response when so many medications are combined or, for that matter, when just two drugs are mixed?

If Jim had just held tight for another day or two instead of coming to the ER when he did, he could probably have convinced himself that the voices were not going to return, and he might have avoided a hospitalization. But then we would not have had the chance to meet this interesting patient and follow him through his brief inpatient stay. And we would have missed the opportunity to figure out why, after all those years being free from auditory hallucinations, he was hearing voices again.

Jim may be the most considerate patient I have worked with in the ER. Even before I had a chance to introduce myself, he told me that he was not in any immediate difficulty and did not need me right away. From Room 11, where he was waiting, he had seen me enter and leave my office often enough to realize how busy I was that evening.

Nothing about Jim's appearance suggested an acute problem. In fact, all the signs pointed to chronicity: his face had the drawn, wasted look often seen on those who have had a serious mental illness for many years. There was expression in that face, but it did not fit the moment. It was as if he had assumed a pleasant grin to see him through all occasions.

Jim was 46. He had been diagnosed with schizophrenia at age 22 and hospitalized at a state institution for three years. The voices he heard when he first became ill were eradicated by Thorazine. He was still on that medication, and was being followed at a mental health clinic. Jim had not been rehospitalized since his first psychotic break. He denied ever using illicit drugs or abusing alcohol. His toxicology screen was negative.

Jim was alert and seemed eager to talk to me. He knew who he was, where he was, and the exact date. He was mildly anxious and somewhat restless. His face continued to wear the same grin I had noticed when I first spotted him from the hallway. In everyday terms, this expression would be called silly. In psychiatry, it is called inappropriate affect and is often seen in patients with chronic schizophrenia.

The conversation flowed normally. There was no sign of formal thought disorder. The thought content was rational. There was no evidence of paranoia. Jim did acknowledge feeling depressed because four days earlier he had started hearing voices again for the first time since he began taking Thorazine nearly a quarter of a century before. The voices were keeping him from sleeping. On his own, he decided one time to take an extra dose of Thorazine at 3 a.m., but this did not stop the voices or restore his sleep.

The voices were telling Jim to hurt himself and others. "They told me to strangle my cat," he said, immediately denying any intention to comply. A voice also said, "The only way you are going to get rid of me is to strangle yourself." He responded to this command only to the extent of putting his hands around his neck. Though he admitted to being bothered by the voices, he assured me he would never act on them.

Jim insisted that he had been taking his medicine as prescribed. He denied any significant recent changes in his life or any new stressors. He insisted that all was well at home. One of his guardians confirmed this when I called her. She added that, during the 14 years she had cared for Jim, she never knew him to hear voices.

I asked Jim if his routine had changed in any way. He said that about five weeks earlier he had started taking Colestid to counteract a high blood level of LDL ("bad") cholesterol. Colestid is a resin that binds bile acids in the intestine, forming a complex there that is excreted in the feces and thus lowering the blood level of "bad" cholesterol. But the resin was aggravating his hemorrhoids, and Jim's physician had decided to switch him from Colestid to Pravachol. Pravachol acts in the liver by inhibiting an enzyme required for cholesterol synthesis. On his doctor's orders, Jim had stopped taking Colestid four days before he came to the ER complaining about the voices. In fact, the voices had stopped earlier that day, but he wanted to be seen because he was afraid they would start again.

I recommended that Jim sign himself into the inpatient psychiatric unit. He readily agreed. Assuming that the auditory hallucinations had returned because Thorazine was no longer effective, the psychiatrist who accepted him told me that he was considering switching the patient to another neuroleptic or to an atypical antipsychotic medication. That strategy seemed reasonable to me. But then, as I was finishing the paperwork for Jim's admission to the psychiatric unit, it suddenly occurred to me that since the only change in the patient's routine was the addition of Colestid, this might have had something to do with the reappearance of the disturbing voices that had been quiet all these years. If Colestid bound to bile acids in the intestine, could it also bind to Thorazine? This would cut the intestinal absorption of Thorazine, reducing the blood level of this drug and ultimately the amount that entered the brain.

I called the psychiatrist and passed on this thought. He agreed to keep the patient on his current dose of Thorazine and wait to see if the voices stayed silent. Three days later, I visited Jim in the inpatient unit. He seemed fine. He happily reported that there had been no more voices, and he was scheduled to be discharged the next day. Ambien had been added to his regimen to help with sleep.

The reappearance of Jim's auditory hallucinations after so many years was almost certainly due to a drug–drug interaction: the binding and excretion of Thorazine by Colestid. The patient might as well have stopped taking his medication. What really happened is that he stopped absorbing it. In all likelihood, four to five days after Jim discontinued

Colestid, the Thorazine that he had been taking all along returned to a therapeutic level, quelling the voices as it had done for so long.

If Jim had just held tight for another day or two instead of coming to the ER when he did, he could probably have convinced himself that the voices were not going to return, and he might have avoided a hospitalization. But then we would not have had the chance to meet this interesting patient and follow him through his brief inpatient stay. And we would have missed the opportunity to figure out why, after all those years being free from auditory hallucinations, he was hearing voices again.

18   How a Stomachache
Turned a Head

Psychiatric patients who take neuroleptic medication sometimes have what is known as a dystonic reaction. The cause is abnormal muscle tone, and the most common symptoms are muscle stiffness, protruding tongue, rolled-back eyes, and twisting of the neck and head. Patients taking neuroleptics are generally given oral Cogentin, Artane, or Benadryl to prevent this side effect. Some patients get dystonic reactions when they stop taking these medications, others when the dose of the neuroleptic is increased. Those with dystonic reactions often come to the ER puzzled and frightened by the sometimes freakish changes in their bodies. An injection of Benadryl or Cogentin usually reverses the dystonia.

He had had severe nausea that afternoon and was given Compazine, a drug with a chemical structure similar to some neuroleptic agents used for patients with schizophrenia and bipolar disorder. He had never taken Compazine before and was not warned of this side effect—a dystonic reaction known as torticollis—where the neck muscles contract and the head twists to one side, usually to the right.

The most memorable dystonic reaction I saw in the ER happened to someone who was not being treated for a psychiatric disorder. I vividly recall the early evening when a well-dressed man in his mid-20s, strapped upright on a gurney, was being pushed by paramedics to Room 1. Several family members accompanied him. He and his entourage seemed shocked to the core by what was happening: the patient's neck and head were twisted hard to the right.

He had had severe nausea that afternoon and was given Compazine, a drug with a chemical structure similar to some neuroleptic agents used in patients with schizophrenia and bipolar disorder. He had never taken Compazine before, and was not warned of this side effect—a dystonic reaction known as torticollis—where the neck muscles contract and the head twists to one side, usually to the right.

Immediately sizing up the situation, someone from the ER staff suggested an injection of Benadryl. A physician assistant who was not involved in the case but who was standing nearby said, "The first-line treatment for dystonic reactions is Cogentin." Nonetheless, the patient was given an injection of Benadryl. Twenty minutes later, he looked straight ahead again and was discharged.

Two hours later, he was back with his family and the same torticollis. The Benadryl had worn off before fully neutralizing the effect of the Compazine and uncontracting the affected neck muscles. The patient's and the family's spirits were low. Their concern was even greater than before. Another injection of Benadryl straightened the patient's head, this time for good. If the attending physician had listened to the physician assistant and written the order for Cogentin instead of Benadryl, the first injection might have done the trick.

19   A Serious Overdose, But of What?

Many patients who come to the ER have taken too much of their own medication, or of someone else's, or have swallowed a substance not intended for human use. The most feared overdoses of high-lethality medications include tricyclic antidepressants (fatal cardiac arrhythmias), lithium (seizure, cardiovascular collapse, and renal failure), and acetaminophen (serious or fatal liver and kidney damage). The most common overdoses occur with medications of low lethality—whether providentially or through calculation is an open question. Even when relatively large amounts of these substances are taken, the result is usually not life-threatening. Still, with some drugs, the outcome can be serious and the symptoms of the overdose difficult to identify.

The lesson to be relearned here involves a crucial point in the practice of medicine: clinicians must be ready to recognize a known syndrome and make the diagnosis—even when all the usual signs and symptoms are not seen—whether the syndrome is due to an illness or a toxic overdose.

It was 5:30 a.m., and I was ready for bed. I had my coat on and was about to leave the ER, when I decided instead to say good-bye to my coworkers, who were facing another hour and a half of work. It had been an easy on-call shift for me—one patient and a quick disposition. I could afford to take a minute for genuine pleasantries.

"I've never seen anything like it. He's completely dissociated. Go take a look." This is what the ER attending said about the patient in Room 6 as I tried to say good-bye.

The patient's right hand had a severe, coarse, irregular tremor. His legs shifted on the mattress, casting off the sheet the nurses repeatedly put back in place to cover him. Half raised up from the gurney and with eyes that looked everywhere but did not seem to recognize anything, he alternately stared into and away from the bright fluorescent light overhead. He did not seem to comprehend what was in his visual field.

Deng, a 21-year-old Chinese man, was short and had thick black hair. Clinicians doing a mental status evaluation would say he was in acute distress. His face had the look of terror. The nurses' efforts to comfort and reassure him helped little, and only momentarily. He acted as if he were in a hostile environment. Repeatedly asked simple questions by the staff, he writhed away from each interlocutor as if his life were at stake. The only sounds he made were brief spews of English or Chinese. Nothing he said was intelligible. He could not tell us about himself or how he came to be in this state. I doubted Deng was dissociating as the attending first suggested. I thought he was delirious.

Deng's mother, brother, cousin, and girlfriend went in and out of Room 6 periodically. They were at a loss to explain what had happened to this person in such obvious distress. The mother spoke no English, and the brother and cousin spoke it only haltingly. The girlfriend left the ER before I could talk to her. Deng had been at her apartment the previous evening. At some point during the early hours of the morning, he became unable to get up from the couch. The girlfriend called his brother, who then brought Deng to the ER.

Deng had never been diagnosed with a mental disorder. But family members told us that he often drank too much alcohol and was depressed about how things were going with his girlfriend. On both forearms, we noticed numerous well-healed slash marks, more extensive than most seen in the ER, and, on his right leg, a new small, curved laceration, still bleeding, that seemed self-inflicted. The consensus was that he had taken an overdose, but of what? Deng was in no position to tell us.

The attending's first thought about the diagnosis was alcohol withdrawal, based on the family's report of Deng's heavy alcohol use. (They could not tell us how much he drank but said they had never heard of

him using illicit drugs.) I recalled that Asians have less alcohol dehydrogenase (ADH) and its polymorphisms, the liver enzymes responsible for
metabolizing alcohol, than Caucasians, and I worried that even a relatively small amount of alcohol here could be doing a lot of damage. But
the blood alcohol test came back negative, as did the tests for drugs of
abuse. We were told that Deng had never had a significant medical problem, was not on medication, and, as far as the family knew, had no access
to anyone else's prescription medication. Currently, he was working as a
cashier in a department store.

Deng's brother brought in several items found in the patient's car.
There was a bottle two-thirds full of thick, grayish liqueur; one full and
one partial six-pack of a herbal formulation in tall, slender bottles; and an
empty box of Maximum Strength Unisom SleepGels (we never did find
the bottle it contained). Recalling that herbal compounds are often
made under poor quality control, the attending worried that a con-
taminant of this liquid, possibly lead, mercury, or arsenic, might be
the toxic agent.

A nurse threaded a nasogastric tube into Deng's stomach, and a
small amount of green, mint-scented liquid was aspirated into a jar.
What was this? We had no clue. Neither the liqueur nor the herbal
compound was green or smelled of mint. It was unlikely that Unisom
would be mint flavored. The initial collective feeling was that an overdose of this sleeping potion would put someone out, but not cause
agitation, tremor, and psychotic-like responses.

Deng had been on a heart monitor from the start. The rhythm
strip showed sinus rhythm, but with tachycardia of 140 to 150 beats
per minute. A 12-lead electrocardiogram (EKG) was normal, except
for the tachycardia. All other vital signs were within normal limits and
stable. The pupils were dilated. There was no fever. Electrolytes and
blood values were unremarkable. A computed axial tomography
(CAT) scan of the head to rule out stroke, tumor, or an infectious focus was also negative.

During the hour following his admission to the ER, Deng's condition remained the same. He still could tell us nothing. The agitation had

not diminished. With no clue to what caused the delirium, the attending was reluctant to medicate him, though intravenous fluid was given. Clearly, Deng would have to be hospitalized. The medical admitting officer (MAO), whose approval was required for admission, as well as a resident, were called to examine him. A bed was reserved in the progressive care unit (PCU).

As with any suspected overdose—and an overdose of something was thought from the start to be the reason for Deng's condition—the Maryland Poison Control Center, a division of the University of Maryland School of Pharmacy, was contacted soon after Deng arrived in the ER. But these experts, so often helpful to us, had no diagnosis. When I left the ER around 6:30 a.m., the ER staff, the MAO, and the resident were still puzzling over the case.

The diagnosis of anticholinergic intoxication was made by the MAO after a second consultation with the Maryland Poison Control Center, before Deng went to the PCU. Deng had most of the symptoms of anticholinergic intoxication, but he did not have a fever and there was no report of dry mouth or dry skin (which may have been overlooked). This kind of poisoning affects both the central nervous system (delirium, agitation, tremor, psychotic-like speech and behavior) and the peripheral nervous system (dilated pupils, tachycardia). The empty Unisom box Deng's brother found in his car was consistent with this diagnosis, since Benadryl is Unisom's active agent.

Later that day, I went to the PCU to see how Deng was doing. He was in a private room, surrounded by the same family members I had met earlier. (The girlfriend was not there. One can only wonder what she was thinking and feeling.) A glance at the heart monitor told me that the tachycardia had resolved. But little else had changed. A nurse said no one was able to communicate with Deng. His brother told the nurse that, when he asked Deng a question, the answer seemed to belong to some other question. Deng mumbled in his delirium about making change for an imagined or recalled customer, as if he were still at his cashier's job.

Intravenous fluid was started in the ER and was continued in the PCU. A single dose of Haldol was given to suppress agitation. Physostigmine, which reversibly inhibits cholinesterases in the periphery and in the CNS, slowing the metabolism of acetylcholine, is sometimes used to break the anticholinergic syndrome, but was not used here.

The PCU staff estimated that Deng had taken about 30 Maximum Strength Unisom SleepGels. A full bottle contains 32 soft gelatin capsules. At 50 mg each, this would be 1500 mg of Benadryl. (The dosage range for Benadryl is 25–50 mg/day.) The green color of the gastric aspirate may have been the result of mixing the blue dye in the SleepGels with other stomach contents. The mint smell was not accounted for.

Around 8 a.m. the next day, about 26 hours after coming to the ER, Deng woke up and asked the nurse, "Where am I?" The delirium had broken, and the patient was now able to talk rationally and in a goal-directed way, though his pupils were still slightly dilated. Symptoms of anticholinergic intoxication usually resolve after this period of time, with peripheral symptoms clearing before CNS symptoms.

A consultation psychiatrist who saw the patient later that day learned the reason for the overdose: Deng wanted to get attention and sympathy from his girlfriend. This was his magical but failed way of trying to improve their troubled relationship. (Wanting attention and attempting to punish others are the most common explanations given by ER patients for self-injurious behavior.) Deng never did acknowledge what medication he had overdosed on, how much he had taken, or whether he had taken anything besides Unisom (tests for acetaminophen and salicylates were negative). He was judged not to be a danger to himself at this point and was discharged with a referral for psychiatric follow-up.

Benadryl, whose generic name is diphenhydramine, is marketed as Unisom and Sominex. This drug is used widely as an antihistamine for allergies, as a sedative hypnotic, and for prophylaxis and treatment of tremors and dystonias in patients taking neuroleptic medication. We see many overdoses in the ER, most gestural and with low morbidity. I have had many patients who overdosed on Benadryl, taken either alone or in combination with other medications. Yet this was the first case of anticholinergic intoxication from Benadryl I had seen in four years of working in the ER. This outcome was very different from a subtoxic overdose, which makes the patient sleepy, but not agitated or delirious. (To paraphrase physician/alchemist Paracelsus [1493–1541], *The dose makes the poison.*) The poison control center estimated that only a fraction of one percent of all reported cases of Benadryl overdose lead to anticholinergic intoxication.

The medical staff working early that Sunday morning and I, as well as the poison control center, were slow to recognize—even with an empty Unisom box as a clue—a presentation of anticholinergic intoxication that did not quite fit the familiar diagnostic mantra "Mad as a hatter; blind as a bat; hot as Hades; dry as a bone; red as a beet." The patient was not febrile. No one from the ER staff reported observing dry mucosa or dry skin. And beet-red flushing would be an unlikely symptom for this patient because of his darker Asian skin.

The lesson to be relearned here involves a crucial point in the practice of medicine: clinicians must be ready to recognize a syndrome and make the diagnosis—even when all the usual signs and symptoms are not seen—whether the syndrome is due to an illness or a toxic overdose.

20 A Closed Head Injury
Leads to Paranoid Psychosis

Irritability, memory loss, anxiety, depression, and a number of other psychiatric disorders are common after traumatic brain injury (TBI), but hallucinations and delusions are rare complications. Some people with head trauma show psychotic symptoms immediately after injury, while others go for years before these symptoms appear. Traumatic brain injury can be either focal or diffuse. Focal injury occurs when blood vessels break and hemorrhage. Diffuse injury is caused when soft brain tissue moves unevenly within the hard skull on impact, twisting and stretching neuronal axons. The damage ranges from a brief physiological disruption of neural circuits to torn axons. This traumatic twisting and tearing of brain circuits is believed to underlie the psychotic emotions, thoughts, and behavior seen in some patients with closed head injury.

About 20 minutes into the interview, John suddenly broke away from our dialogue. Aware of how much the "responding to internal stimuli" cliché is overused in clinical practice, I was nonetheless convinced that this patient really was caught up in a competing reality. "Someone just shot my wife, my whole family," John insisted a voice had just told him. He was visibly upset by the news.

John, 48, was brought to the ER by his wife. While she was driving him home from his job, John broke down crying, convinced that the voices he had been hearing posed a serious threat to him and his family. Earlier that day, he had deliberately stepped on an electric hot cable at the parking garage where he worked as an attendant, hoping that this dangerous action would somehow ward off the threat that now loomed ominous.

Seven weeks before, while playing pool, John fell and hit the back of his head hard on an old iron radiator. He did not lose consciousness but felt woozy and disoriented. Soon after, he began having severe headaches that were not relieved by Tylenol and were serious enough for him to consult his primary-care physician. This doctor told John, "You think too much, that's why you have headaches." John was deeply upset by the doctor's cavalier and callous disregard of his pain.

Three weeks after the fall, John's wife noticed significant changes in his personality and behavior. He became distant and paranoid and, as she put it, "talked out of his head" intermittently. "If I tell you something, don't look at me like I'm crazy," John said to prepare his wife before revealing, "I hear these voices in my mind." The voices told him that someone named Dave was at the center of a conspiracy determined to destroy John and his family. John wrote down some of the messages he had received from the voices. What his wife read frightened her, and she threw the paper out because she could not stand to have this reminder of what her husband was experiencing.

John stopped eating after the voices told him that "something was in the food." He lost weight and tried to hide this by wearing additional clothes. A religious man, John was observed by his wife holding up a table in a menacing way, as if against an imagined presence, and saying, "Before I let you hurt my family, I will kill you first." One week before coming to the ER, a voice told John that Dave had just jumped off the porch of their third-floor apartment. Convinced this had happened, he passed the news on to his wife. John was also observed talking to the fish in their aquarium.

In the ER, John's memory for recent and past events was intact. He was tall, thin, and gaunt and looked worried. Calm and cooperative after an injection of Haldol, he kept his eyes closed for much of the interview. John denied feeling depressed but said he was "mad as hell" at Dave, who he claimed had put "spray" on him at home, on the bus, and at work, causing him to hear voices. He denied visual hallucinations.

About 20 minutes into the interview, John suddenly broke away from our dialogue. Aware of how much the "responding to internal stimuli" cliché is overused in clinical practice, I was nonetheless convinced that this patient really was caught up in a competing reality. "Someone just shot my wife, my whole family," John insisted a voice had just told him. He was visibly upset by the news. He told me that he had stepped on the hot cable at the parking garage earlier that day, intending to kill himself, because he believed, "Everyone else in my family would be okay if I died." Clearly, John felt responsible for putting his family in the danger he imagined Dave was posing.

John had not previously been diagnosed with or treated for a mental disorder. He had used heroin, cocaine, and marijuana for several years, sporadically and in small amounts. He reported drinking alcohol, heavily at times, during the previous 18 months, but had not used illicit drugs or alcohol for two weeks before coming to the ER. The toxicology screen was negative. John had stopped using drugs and alcohol many times before his traumatic brain injury (TBI) without experiencing paranoid auditory hallucinations or paranoid delusions; withdrawal seemed an unlikely cause of his psychotic symptoms. A noncontrast computed tomography (CT) scan of the head done in the ER was normal.

When I first suggested to John that he needed to be hospitalized, he agreed, saying, "I thought that would be necessary." But when I asked him to sign the voluntary admission form, he refused. He also refused to answer any more questions and became guarded and irritable. John put on his clothes and tried to leave the ER. Security was called. He was given another injection of Haldol, which took the edge off his agitation. John's wife and a nurse helped me to convince him to sign himself into the hospital voluntarily.

John was hospitalized for six days. He was started on Risperdal. Relying, I assume, on the patient's self-report, the attending psychiatrist told me that John's psychotic symptoms appeared to diminish. John became less suspicious and paranoid, and he told a nurse in the unit that he considered the voices a "test." Then, inexplicably, John denied to the inpatient staff having had the previously acknowledged experiences and asked to be discharged. John's wife told me that her husband seemed less troubled during his hospitalization but was not aware of how he had changed since his head injury. While in the unit, he showed no epileptic signs or symptoms. An electroencephalogram (EEG) was normal.

After discharge, John's psychiatrist doubled the dose of Risperdal because the auditory hallucinations and paranoid thinking persisted. As far as I can determine, he was never free of these symptoms after the TBI. Seven months later, John was hospitalized a second time for one week for what his wife described as "another breakdown." John attributed this relapse, in part, to using heroin again. Shortly after the second hospitalization, he stopped keeping outpatient appointments and stopped taking medication.

A year after I evaluated John in the ER, I spoke to him and his wife by phone. I asked if Risperdal had helped with the voices. John said it made them worse. Standard neuroleptics sometimes slow the recovery of neurocognitive function in patients with TBI and have even been known to (paradoxically) cause psychotic symptoms. Neuroleptics can promote seizures in patients who are prone to them, presumably by lowering the threshold for achieving the electrical discharge that drives seizures. This electrical discharge has itself been associated with psychotic symptoms. The jury is still out on the effect of atypical antipsychotics like Risperdal for patients with TBI. In the ER, John had insisted that drinking beer was the only remedy he knew that helped with the voices.

At the time I called, John was not taking any medication or seeing any mental health clinician. He claimed he could not afford the copayments on the bills he had already received. He did not have insurance, but his wife's insurance covered outpatient visits to the psychiatrist he had previously seen. I encouraged John to recontact his former psychiatrist. I also gave him the name of another psychiatrist who specializes in treating psychotic disorders.

John's paranoid auditory hallucinations and paranoid delusions were constant and bothersome and interfered with his sleep. I tried to pin him down on what the voices were saying. "Don't go to work" was the only clear message I was able to hear from the imprecise answers he gave to my repeated questions about his psychotic thoughts and feelings. He also reported what he called a "sticking feeling" in his head, a pain that felt like a sharp object penetrating his skull.

Everything John said seemed vague and spacey. He had little purchase on his world and little insight into it. He had been let go from his job, which he had held for two years before the head injury, because the voices interfered with his work. He was now parking cars at another lot, just three hours a day, because that was all the work he could handle. The family was sinking into debt. I could only imagine what other pressures John's psychosis were putting on his wife and son, who lived at home.

From the muddle of John's replies to my questions, I could glean that the voices were still threatening his family. "I try not to pay attention," he said, but obviously he was not succeeding at distancing himself from the hallucinatory taunts. I asked if the voices ever made him feel like harming himself or anyone else (after all, they were threatening him and his family). John denied this. "I'm a religious man," he told me, as if religion would curb any impulse he might have to retaliate. During our ER interview, John said he was "mad" at the voices and at Dave. He had tried to talk to the voices but had no intention or plan to harm Dave.

John seemed more concerned about his church and his family than about himself. He did not complain about how his life had gone downhill so drastically since he had hit his head on a radiator. I did not doubt that the paranoid auditory hallucinations and paranoid delusions John reported were genuine. I had no suspicion that he was malingering; he had neither the guile nor the sophistication needed to create and maintain such a fabrication. If anything, he minimized his illness and the effect it was having on his life.

John's voice sounded flat. I did not ask if he felt depressed (I should have), but he said nothing to indicate that he was. I suspect he was depressed but lacked the insight to express his feelings. He told me he had not used heroin since his second hospitalization and drank only an occasional beer. John was not doing well.

Most patients with a mild TBI are doing well one year later, but 10 to 20 percent have persistent symptoms. The temporal association between John's injury and the onset of psychotic symptoms—absent before the injury—is consistent with, but does not fully establish, causality. Ideally, one would like to be able to link the neuropathology of the injury to a neuroanatomical model of psychosis.

There are two kinds of consequences from TBI: focal, with severe bleeding; and diffuse, which usually does not involve hemorrhage, and can include a lesion known as diffuse axonal injury. According to T. W. McAllister, "The most common diffuse injuries . . . result from the differential motion of the brain within the skull. Stretching and twisting of neuronal axons produce a spectrum of injuries to the axon, ranging from brief physiologic disruption of function without obvious autonomic disruption to widespread neuronal tearing." Neither kind of lesion is likely to show up on a CT scan or an EEG. John's were both negative.

Injuries to one side of the head often produce lesions on or near the opposite side of the brain, which may slam into the hard dura on impact. John's occipital (back of the head) trauma could have damaged the axons of his frontal lobes, which lie under the dura of the front head. Many of his symptoms are those seen in frontal lobe syndrome. If the back of John's head was rotating when it hit the radiator, that impact may have caused a twisting of the brain within the cranium, causing diffuse axonal shearing and tearing.

The reasons most often cited for poor outcome after a TBI are a history of prior mild head trauma, prior psychiatric symptoms, and age over 40. John's wife told me that, two years before he hit his head on the radiator, she had hit him in the head with a monkey wrench. (She did not say why; I did not ask.) The 48-year-old John, who was not doing well, had two of the three known risk factors for poor outcome.

One year after his head injury, John met all the *DSM-IV* criteria for the diagnosis of paranoid schizophrenia, except for the general medical condition exclusion. His diagnosis was psychotic disorder due to a medical condition (TBI).

From all the contradictory biopsychiatric data accumulated on the aberrations in brain structure and function in schizophrenic patients, the most robust conclusion is that schizophrenia is a brain disease caused by synaptic misconnections that occur during abnormal neurodevelopment. Considering the similarity between the psychotic symptoms that sometimes follow TBI and the symptoms of schizophrenia, it is tempting to ask if brain lesions caused by this kind of trauma create a similar, aberrant brain circuitry. In this model, traumatic injury to vulnerable and critical brain structures would cause abnormal neural communication similar to that attributed to misconnected neurons in schizophrenia. Both lesions would, in effect, become the biological substrates for feeling, thinking, and behavior that psychiatry labels psychotic.

21   A Patient Who Risked Death Trying to Drown His Hiccups

Most people, including those diagnosed with a mental disorder, do not get into trouble by drinking excessive amounts of the earth's most abundant liquid, water. But a small percentage of schizophrenic patients, as well as a still smaller number of persons without this disorder, do. Psychogenic polydipsia (psychologically motivated excessive drinking of fluid) is the diagnosis given to those persons who may drink up to 12 liters of fluid a day. When Mark Twain quipped, "Water, taken in moderation, cannot hurt anybody," he was not thinking of these patients.

Some who worked with Nick saw the problem as medical; others were equally convinced that it was psychiatric. So, for three years, Nick was in and out of the hospital, playing a dangerous game of tag with death.

Some people who drink large amounts of water are unable to metabolize the excess, which is then taken up by the blood, causing a dilution of serum sodium. This condition is known as hyponatremia, or low sodium concentration in the blood.

The dilution of serum sodium causes a perturbation of water balance in brain cells, so that more water flows from inside the cellular space to outside than is normal in the proper functioning of these cells. Accumulation of water in the interstitial spaces outside the cells causes the brain to swell and press against the inside of the dura, the rock-hard skull. The degree of brain swelling depends on both how low and how fast the serum sodium level falls. Given sufficient time, other substrates within the cell can diffuse outward, reducing the flow of water from the cell driven by low serum sodium. Brain swelling beyond a certain point can perturb normal electrical function and cause a seizure. This is often the symptom that brings the patient to the ER.

Most patients with psychogenic polydipsia and hyponatremia come for treatment before reaching this degree of acuity. They present with changes in mental status (confusion, disorientation) and muscle cramps, the early central and peripheral signs of altered water balance.

Between July 1993 and May 1996, Nick was seen in the ER 94 times. He was hospitalized 31 times. He spent 104 days in the hospital. Eighty-four of those days were spent in various medical units, 20 in the psychiatric unit. The total cost of these services was more than $110,000.

In spite of the many hours I worked ER shifts around the clock, and in spite of Nick's frequent appearances there, I was never asked to evaluate him. We must have just missed each other. But Nick was an ER legend, and I would often hear the staff discussing his seemingly intractable case. The nurses were worried about Nick. In particular, they were worried that he would die from the effects of drinking too much water.

One night as I was finishing an evening shift, the overnight charge nurse asked me, in a tone tinged with despair, "Would you try to do something about this?" She could not have known that I had prior experience with psychogenic polydipsia and hyponatremia, as well as an ongoing clinical and theoretical interest in this disorder.

Between 1989 and 1991, I was a research associate in the Department of Psychiatry at the University of Maryland School of Medicine. I worked on a research protocol designed to determine whether 2 cc intramuscular injections of the neuroleptic Prolixin Decanoate, traditionally given to schizophrenic patients every two weeks, could be given with the same or better overall efficacy every six weeks instead. Medications at lower doses usually cause fewer, and less severe, side effects, an important consideration in the treatment of patients with a chronic mental disorder. The study was conducted with outpatients in a community mental health center.

One of our patients, an obese 32-year-old man, relapsed on the lower dose of Prolixin Decanoate. His mother, with whom he lived, told us that he was more withdrawn than usual, was not sleeping, and was drinking excessive amounts of fluids. He was hospitalized in an inpatient psychiatric unit for 24 days. While in the hospital, the patient was diagnosed with hypertension (150/90 mm Hg) and was started on the diuretic hydrochlorothiazide, 50 mg daily. He continued the Prolixin Decanoate injections, supplemented with oral Prolixin.

Three weeks after the patient was discharged from the hospital, his mother found the patient in bed, diaphoretic, mute, and seizing. In the ER, the patient's serum sodium level was 108 mEq/L (normal range, 134–146 mEq/L). He was treated with three-percent normal saline and admitted to intensive care. He made a full recovery, without any sign of neurological damage. Hydrochlorothiazide was discontinued, and Capoten (25 mg three times daily) was substituted to control hypertension.

The patient's mother reported that, during the week before her son's second hospitalization, he had been drinking three to four quarts of beer and up to six liters of soft drinks daily. Though he had been drinking excessive amounts of fluids for some time and had probably been mildly hyponatremic, he was not diagnosed with symptomatic hyponatremia until he was brought to the ER after his seizure.

The hydrochlorothiazide the patient received during his first hospitalization lowers blood pressure by reducing plasma volume through diuresis but depletes sodium as well. The combined effects of polydipsia (causing an increase in blood volume and consequent dilution of sodium in the blood) and the loss of sodium through the kidney (caused by the diuretic) in all likelihood drove his serum sodium level low enough to cause severe hyponatremia (108 mEq/L) and a seizure. If his mother had not found him when she did and called 911, the patient probably would have died.

I reported this case in a letter to the *American Journal of Psychiatry*. The report concludes with this caveat: "Excess water consumed by polydipsic schizophrenic patients should be considered a 'drug' in a potential drug-drug interaction with any substance that alters water balance. The polydipsia diagnosis should be conspicuously noted in the charts of such patients, and a warning about prescribing thiazide diuretics should appear." Clearly, the physician who prescribed hydrochlorothiazide for our patient while he was in the psychiatric unit was not aware of his polydipsia. Neither was any of us who were involved with his treatment at the outpatient clinic.

I have never forgotten how close this patient came to dying. So, when the charge nurse asked me to "do something" about Nick, I felt I had to try. I started with his medical records. Reading Nick's charts soon became mind-numbing: ER, hospitalization, discharge . . . ER, hospitalization, discharge . . . ER . . . The presentations were essentially identical.

Nick would come to the ER, sometimes on his own but most often by ambulance. He would tell the triage nurse that he was there "to get help with the hiccups," which were out of control and causing him considerable discomfort. Without intervention at this point, Nick would have continued to drink water with the expectation— proven wrong many times—that if he could just drink enough water the hiccups would stop.

Nick came to the ER in various stages of confusion and disorientation. He complained of leg cramps and nausea. His serum sodium level was usually between 110 and 127 mEq/L (normal range, 134–146 mEq/L). Several times, he came in seizing, an indication that the fluid balance in his brain cells had changed so that the brain was swelling and pressing against the hard surface of the skull. Three times he required intubation.

To correct the hyponatremia, Nick was started on hypertonic saline in the ER and then sent to the intensive care unit (ICU). From there he went to a medical floor. With saline infusion, forced fluid restriction, and diuresis, his serum sodium level stabilized within the normal range after two or three days.

Usually, that is. Nick became highly inventive at circumventing the measures the staff devised to restrict his fluid intake. When the faucets in his hospital room were shut off, he drank from the toilet. On one occasion, when he came to the ER with a serum sodium level of 117 mEq/L and was treated in the usual way, he was found seizing on the floor of his hospital room. The serum sodium level was 99 mEq/L! That was a close call.

Why? That is the question everyone familiar with Nick's case asks. Why would someone continue to do something so destructive, and sabotage the efforts of so many people who were trying to help him overcome a behavior that was compromising—and threatening—his life?

Nick was one of the least insightful patients I have ever known. He had an IQ of 84, which put him at the lower end of normal intelligence. He had never married and lived with his mother and father in a house not far from the hospital. As far as I know, the only explanation Nick has ever given for his excessive fluid intake is, "I drink to drown the hiccups." Many years earlier, a friend had suggested this remedy to him. In spite of all the evidence to the contrary, Nick continued to act as if he believed that this was the way to handle the problem. The irony that further water drinking made the hiccups worse was lost on him. He told me that when his hiccups became severe he drank between two and five gallons of water daily.

The hiccups began in 1983 while he was in the army, stationed in Beirut, Lebanon, and had plagued him ever since. It was noted in Nick's records that he did not drink fluids excessively until the hiccups started. The pattern was that he stopped hiccupping when his serum sodium level became normal, near the end of a hospital stay. For a time after discharge, he would reduce his fluid intake, and the hiccups were either suppressed or became mild and tolerable.

As far as I could tell, Nick either drank more water and the hiccups became worse, or the hiccups became worse and he drank more water to "drown" them. Perhaps the situation was not entirely one way or the other. With his low IQ and lack of insight, both sides of this dichotomy may have synchronously come into play. We may never understand Nick's behavior any better than we do now. Ultimately, the psychopathological and the irrational appear to converge here in a mystery.

Unlike many persons with psychogenic polydipsia and hyponatremia, Nick was not diagnosed with schizophrenia or a schizophrenia spectrum disorder. (Over a period of three years in the ER, I saw at least six schizophrenic patients with chronic hyponatremia, but their cases were far less serious than Nick's.) For a time, it was thought that Nick's excessive water drinking may have been due to obsessive compulsive disorder (OCD). He was given Anafranil, without effect. Later, the OCD diagnosis was revoked. At various times, Nick took Elavil and Prozac for depression, with little obvious improvement. During one psychiatric evaluation, he was given the diagnosis of dependent personality disorder.

No medical reason could be found for Nick's hiccupping or hyponatremia. His evaluation for the syndrome of inappropriate secretion of antidiuretic hormone (SIADH), one of the most common causes of hyponatremia, was negative. Computed axial tomography (CAT) and magnetic resonance imaging (MRI) scans of the head were unremarkable. In 1994, Nick had a laparoscopic fundoplication (a surgical procedure in which the bottom part of the stomach is sutured to the esophagus) to repair a hiatal hernia that was causing esophageal reflux. This condition was felt not to have contributed to the chronic hiccups. Nick did not smoke cigarettes or use illicit drugs and had not used alcohol for six years.

It should come as no surprise that, as Nick continued to come to the ER and was repeatedly admitted to the hospital over a period of three years, concern rose in the departments of emergency medicine, internal medicine, and psychiatry, as well as in the other departments that were asked for consults. All strategies failed.

Which brings us back to May 1996, when a charge nurse asked me, "Would you try to do something about this?" Not long after reading Nick's hospital records, I went through the rather large collection of journal articles on psychogenic polydipsia and hyponatremia that I had been accumulating for several years. I found a letter by F. C. Ramirez and D. Y. Graham in the *Annals of Internal Medicine* with the title "Hiccups, Compulsive Water Drinking, and Hyponatremia." The first sentence read, "We report the use of the gamma-aminobutyric acid [GABA] analog baclofen in the prevention of symptomatic hyponatremia caused by compulsive water drinking associated with intractable hiccup."

Like Nick, the patient in question, a 58-year-old man, "drank large volumes of water with the aim of stopping his hiccup." He, too, had multiple hospital admissions (seven over a nine-month period) for symptomatic hyponatremia. The lowest serum sodium level on admission was 99 mEq/L—the level of Nick's serum sodium when he was found seizing on the floor of his hospital room.

Hiccup, with its distinctive sound, is a sudden spasm of the diaphragm causing an inhalation that is involuntarily terminated by an abrupt closing of the glotis, the opening between the vocal cords. This spasm, considered a gastrointestinal reflex distinct from the mechanism underlying normal, rhythmic breathing, is thought to originate through projections from the brain stem that are transmitted at the level of the spine. Anxiety and stress most likely lower the threshold of initiation of this reflex.

Baclofen is a muscle relaxant and antispasticity agent. It acts mainly in the spinal cord by enhancing the neurotransmission of gamma-aminobutyric acid (GABA), the principal inhibitory pathway in the central nervous system. Since the involuntary spasms of the diaphragmatic muscles that cause hiccups are thought to be modulated through the spinal cord, baclofen seemed a rational choice for treatment of this disorder.

On 80 mg of baclofen (20 mg four times daily), Ramirez and Graham's patient no longer drank water to the point where he became severely hyponatremic and had to be hospitalized. The hiccups were not entirely eliminated, but their frequency and intensity were greatly reduced.

I gave a copy of this report to the internal medicine resident who had just begun working in the outpatient clinic where Nick had been followed by a number of clinicians for some time. She started him on baclofen and increased the dose to 60 mg (20 mg three times daily). She instructed him to drink Gatorade instead of water and arranged for the hospital to supply him with this sodium-enriched hydrating fluid. She also arranged for a nurse to visit him regularly at home. Nick had a standing appointment to see this resident every three weeks at the clinic. She periodically called him at home to offer encouragement and monitor his compliance with the protocol of medication and behavior modification that she had set up. Nick's course was remarkably similar to that of the patient described by Ramirez and Graham; the baclofen had an almost immediate effect on reducing his hiccups and compulsive fluid drinking.

Six weeks after baclofen was started and the behavior modification protocol started, I called Nick's mother. "He is doing a whole lot better," she told me. "He still has hiccups, but less often and less severely. He hasn't been hospitalized for six weeks. He's going to see the doctor at the clinic every three weeks now. The hiccups come and go, but he controls them better. He has good days and bad days. This morning, he had hiccups for a half hour. I've seen a tremendous improvement. He's drinking three to four 32-ounce bottles of Gatorade a day now. He used to drink four to five 32-ounce bottles of water an hour." Nick's mother added that her son did not seem confused or disoriented and did not have muscle cramps in his legs—all signs of a diminution of the severe hyponatremia he had had periodically for so long.

In the six-month period after starting the new treatment regimen, Nick had only three ER visits. He was discharged after two of the visits and hospitalized after the third because of a serum sodium level low enough to require saline infusion. We did not find out how or why this relapse had happened. Nick was compliant with his medication, kept his clinic appointments with the resident, and stuck to the rules set for the control of his fluid intake. During the 18 months after this six-month period, he did not come to the ER at all and was not hospitalized.

Besides baclofen, as an adjunct medication for hiccups, Nick took Thorazine (which he had been taking for many years with only marginal benefit), Prozac for a depression spectrum disorder, and Prilosec for a stomach ulcer.

For three years, before starting baclofen and a behavior modification program, Nick fell between the cracks of a modern hospital's departmental system. The ER fulfilled its obligation to initiate treatment for hyponatremia by admitting him to the ICU to correct his low serum sodium. Before being discharged from the hospital, Nick was warned that he would be jeopardizing his life if he continued to drink excessive amounts of water. He was given suggestions about how to avoid this destructive behavior, all to no avail. Nick also spent time in the psychiatric unit, but no intervention made there had any lasting positive effect either.

Some who worked with Nick saw the problem as medical; others were equally convinced that it was psychiatric. So, for three years, Nick was in and out of the hospital, playing a dangerous game of tag with death.

22 Delirium Missed as the Reason for Psychotic Symptoms

"This isn't Sylvia. This is someone the agency sent." So said the 93-year-old man sitting in a wheelchair with his considerably younger wife, Sylvia, standing at his side. Two years earlier, the same man was reading *The New York Times* every day and *The New Yorker* every week. But then his kidneys failed, and he started dialysis. There were problems with hydration and abnormal electrolytes. His concentration was good some times but not other times. Familiar surroundings became unfamiliar. Then he did not recognize his wife. This formerly vigorous, mentally active man was now suffering from delirium, a consequence of his kidney failure and the interventions used to treat it.

The brief but revealing exchange between Sylvia and her husband did not happen in a medical setting, but in the hallway of an apartment building where I lived. Sylvia wanted me to see firsthand what delirium had done to her husband. When delirious patients come to the ER, the cause of their problem is not always recognized.

It is ER protocol to medically clear a patient—to determine that a medical condition is not causing the observed changes in mental status—before asking for a psychiatric consultation. With delirium, however, the line we try to draw between what is medical and what is psychiatric does not hold: the "psychiatric" symptoms that are part and parcel of this disorder are clearly due to a disordered physiology of the central nervous system.

A 35-year-old Indian woman was brought to the ER by ambulance from her home, where she lived with her husband and three children. The paramedics reported that she was incoherent and gave contradictory answers to their questions. Twice earlier that day, neighbors had called emergency medical services (EMS) because of an ongoing domestic disturbance. The husband was intoxicated and did not give the paramedics any useful information about his wife.

Indira told the triage nurse that she was five months pregnant. A note appended to the chart told us that she had been prescribed Synthroid for hypothyroidism, hydrochlorothiazide for hypertension, and Risperdal for reasons not stated.

When an intravenous line was attached to Indira's heparin lock (a needle fused to a flange embedded in a vein), she became frightened and told the nurse that the flexible tube hanging over her was a snake. Indira's report of being five months pregnant was belied by a negative pregnancy test and the fact that she was having her period. Obviously, she was delusional on this point.

Indira was overweight, looked unkempt, and had a significant body odor. It soon became evident that she was not going to tell me much verbally, despite her willingness to cooperate. Indira's voice was low, and her speech was slurred. Though I spoke slowly and used the simplest words, she did not seem to understand many of my questions. Her facial expression alternated between stunned blankness and smiles that did not match the content of the dialogue. I felt certain that Indira's less than fluent English was not the main reason for her inability to relate to her surroundings and to communicate with me.

Indira told me her name and the name of the city in India where she was born. She did not, however, have any idea where she was as we spoke. Asked to name the year, she gave several (none correct). Indira knew her age but gave widely disparate years of birth (all incorrect). Even after looking at the clock on the wall, she could not tell me the time. Asked to simulate the face of a clock by drawing the numbers 1 to 12 in a circle provided her, Indira wrote the numbers in two vertical columns inside the circle. Given a circle numbered like the face of a clock and asked to draw a small hand and a large hand to indicate a specific time, she was flummoxed. It was obvious that this young woman did not have a clear sensorium.

Indira acknowledged feeling depressed, though she could not say why. Her appetite was normal, but her sleep had been markedly reduced for a period of time that she could not specify. I was unable to determine if she was having any psychotic experiences other than those involving the "snake" and her pregnancy. After much prodding, Indira told me that she had recently been admitted to a psychiatric unit at a nearby hospital, but she did not know where, when, or why. Nor could she tell me if she was under any current psychiatric care. She did not know her psychiatric diagnosis or why she was being prescribed Risperdal. She could not tell me if she was taking any or all of her medications. My repeated calls and voicemail messages to her husband were not answered. Since I was seeing Indira between 3 and 4:30 a.m., I had little hope of getting any information from the hospital where she had had the psychiatric admission. I had no way of finding out what Indira had been like before she became ill.

It soon became apparent to me that Indira was delirious, but I did not know why. The ER attending agreed that she needed to go to a medical bed.

In the ER, Indira's chemistry panel was notable for hypokalemia (3.0 mmol/L) and hyperglycemia (163 mg/dL). The alkaline phosphatase level was 193 U/L, the aspartate aminotransferase (AST) level was 95 U/L, and the alanine aminotransferase (ALT) level was 142 U/L—all elevated. The hematology panel values were within normal limits. A noncontrast computed tomography (CT) scan of the head showed no abnormalities. The toxicology screen was negative for alcohol and drugs of abuse.

On her second day in the hospital, Indira was seen by a psychiatrist, who noted that she was confused and disoriented. She rambled on about not being loved and claimed that her food was poisoned. The psychiatrist had not been able to contact the husband or any other family members. He did learn that, during a one-week psychiatric hospitalization five months earlier, Indira had reported seeing snakes and rats and expressed paranoid thoughts. The discharge diagnosis was major depression with psychotic features, rule out schizophrenia. Risperdal was prescribed.

The most striking finding from this hospitalization was that Indira's thyroid stimulating hormone (TSH) level was 47 mIU/mL—*10 times* the upper limit of normal (range, 0.49–4.67 mIU/mL). Severe endocrine imbalance is known to cause both delirium and depression. Indira had most likely not been taking her Synthroid, and she was restarted on this medication in the hospital. Inexplicably, only her initial TSH level was recorded in the chart; there was no way for me to know how Indira had responded to the hormone replacement while she was hospitalized. During a medical admission to the same hospital six months earlier, when symptoms of delirium were also present, her TSH level had been 226 mIU/mL.

Indira's hepatitis panel was negative. The reason for the elevated liver enzymes was not found, but Risperdal was considered to be a possible cause, and it was discontinued in favor of Zyprexa. In 1988, Denis F. Darko and his colleagues at the Veterans Administration Medical Center in San Diego reported a case of severe hypothyroidism (TSH, 353 mIU/mL) with psychotic features, attributed to autoimmune chronic lymphocyticthyroiditis, where the patient's levels of AST and ALT were elevated. This increase in liver enzyme activity is common, though not universal, in severe hypothyroidism. Enzyme levels returned to normal in Darko's patient following metabolic correction with Synthroid.

After spending three days in a medical bed, Indira was transferred to a psychiatric unit at another hospital.

Much Delirium Is Missed

The ER attending who called me to evaluate Indira had missed the delirium diagnosis. In 1995, L. M. Lewis and his colleagues at the St. Louis University Health Sciences Center published an article in *The American Journal of Emergency Medicine* showing that physicians in an urban teaching hospital ER had correctly identified only 17 percent of geriatric patients ultimately determined to have delirium. Philip R. Slavney, Professor of Psychiatry at Johns Hopkins, has compiled a fine descriptive phenomenology of delirium and provided a practical guide for differential diagnosis and treatment in his book *Psychiatric Dimensions of Medical Practice*. "Most often," he points out, "delirium is not recognized because it is not considered."

As the Lewis study showed, even with geriatric patients in the ER, where the suspicion should be high, many delirium cases are missed. The delirium I have seen in the ER has been due mostly to hyponatremia, anticholinergic toxicity, hypoglycemia, alcohol withdrawal, and tetra-hydrocannabinol (THC) intoxication. Patients who become delirious because of hyponatremia, anticholinergic toxicity, hypoglycemia, or alcohol withdrawal require medical hospitalization. Those with THC intoxication who are otherwise medically stable can go to a psychiatric unit.

The *DSM-IV* has set these criteria for the diagnosis of delirium:

A. Disturbance of consciousness (i.e., reduced clarity of awareness of the environment) with reduced ability to focus, sustain or shift attention.

B. A change in cognition (such as memory deficit, disorientation, language disturbance) or the development of a perceptual disturbance [including delusions and hallucinations] that is not better accounted for by a preexisting, established, or evolving dementia.

C. The disturbance develops over a short period of time (usually hours to days) and tends to fluctuate during the course of the day.

D. There is evidence from the history, physical examination, or laboratory findings that the disturbance is caused by the direct physiological consequences of a general medical condition.

Delirium is a derangement of central nervous system physiology that clouds consciousness and breaks a person's link to the environment. Perception is usually affected, and neutral elements in the visual field may be perceived as threatening. A delirious patient seems radically different from his or her regular self—confused, strange, inaccessible, and often "out of it." The easy give-and-take of normal conversation is impossible.

A hallmark of delirium is that the symptoms of the enduring syndrome come and go. This characteristic waxing and waning can make the diagnosis elusive, since any intermittent problem is harder to nail down. Clinicians seeing a delirious patient at different times can see that patient with or without the symptoms of an altered state, which are often worse at night than during the day. Ultimately, it is the level of consciousness that fluctuates, and this may follow changes in the degree of physiological derangement.

Many different physiological stressors have a final common pathway leading to delirium. A partial list would include medications, overdoses of medication, withdrawal from alcohol, benzodiazepines or barbiturates, metabolic abnormalities, infections, vascular disorders, and surgery. Anticholinergic medications are notorious offenders, particularly in patients who are elderly or medically compromised. Ironically—sadly—many cases of delirium in this population are iatrogenic.

It is ER protocol to medically clear a patient—to determine that a medical condition is not causing the observed changes in mental status—before asking for a psychiatric consultation. With delirium, however, the line we try to draw between what is medical and what is psychiatric does not hold: the "psychiatric" symptoms that are part and parcel of this disorder are clearly due to a disordered physiology of the central nervous system.

Differential Diagnosis

As is often the case in medicine, a correct diagnosis of delirium depends on a correct differential diagnosis. Indira was referred to me because of psychiatric symptoms that included disorientation, withdrawal, depression, paranoia, distortions in visual perception, and delusions.

When Indira was hospitalized in an inpatient psychiatric unit five months before I saw her in the ER, she was diagnosed—incorrectly, I believe—with major depression with psychotic features. In our interview, she reported and physically manifested many of the symptoms of major depression: feelings of sadness, loss of interest in her surroundings, apathy, lethargy, decreased sleep, helplessness, and an affect that was alternately sad and inappropriate.

Indira's profound disturbance of consciousness, including a lack of orientation to time and place, is not characteristic even of severe depression but is common in delirium. Because she could give me only the most general facts about her recent and past life, and because there was little collateral information, I was unable to determine the course of onset of her depression. Indira's daughter told the paramedics that her mother had been "like this"—essentially "out of it"—three times in the previous month. Waxing and waning of symptoms is characteristic of delirium, but not of depression, which may have been a direct physiological consequence of her marked hypothyroidism.

While hospitalized five months earlier, Indira was paranoid and reported visual hallucinations. Her discharge diagnosis included a rule-out of schizophrenia. During our ER evaluation, Indira had, at a minimum, what would have to be considered a sensory distortion (the IV line seen as a snake). She was also delusional (she thought she was pregnant in spite of having her period). These deviations from consensually validated reality can be symptoms of schizophrenia, and that diagnosis, along with other psychotic disorders, must be considered.

It could be argued that, during the previous month, Indira's psychotic symptoms came and went depending on whether or not she was taking her antipsychotic medication. But, of all the patients I have seen with decompensated schizophrenia, I cannot recall even one with the kind of visual distortion Indira had. Auditory hallucinations are the rule with schizophrenics in relapse, and often at their baseline as well. Indira's report of seeing a snake is more consistent with delirium than with schizophrenia. Patients in withdrawal from alcohol, benzodiazepines, or barbiturates also have distortions of visual perception, but there is no evidence that Indira abused any of these substances.

The diagnosis that best accounts for Indira's symptoms is delirium due to hypothyroidism. In 1949, R. Asher published a landmark article in the *British Medical Journal* describing 14 cases of hypothyroidism. He used the term *myxoedematous madness* to name the often sudden, sometimes dramatic changes in mental status that can accompany hypothyroidism as severe as Indira's. Myxedema, a hard, nonpitting swelling of subcutaneous tissue, has become a synecdochic synonym for this endocrine derangement. Indira's psychiatric symptoms were classic myxedema madness. Her habitus, too, fit the profile: a puffy and apathetic face, a flabby and flaccid body, a lumbering walk.

If Indira's confusion, disorientation, visual distortions, and delusions resolved after Synthroid was restarted and a euthyroid state was achieved, the delirium-myxedema diagnosis would be all but confirmed. If not, further exploration of her psychiatric symptoms would be necessary. As Slavney pointed out, "As far as psychiatric disorders are concerned, delirium trumps everything." On the other hand, if Indira's thyroid function did not normalize with Synthroid, a further endocrinological workup would be necessary. Severe hypothyroidism like Indira's should be treated aggressively, because prolonged endocrinopathies take their toll on brain neurons. Asher noted in his 1949 article, "The longer the myxoedema is left untreated the poorer is the outlook for recovery."

A Patient from the Medical Literature

Delirium has two faces, which have opposite polarities of altered consciousness and behavior. A delirious patient may be alternately hypoactive and hypoalert, and hyperactive and hyperalert. When I saw Indira in the ER, she typified the hypoactive-hypoalert type—she was quiet, passive, and willing to participate in the interview.

Dara, whose ER evaluation and subsequent hospitalization were reported in the Case Records of the Massachusetts General Hospital in *The New England Journal of Medicine*, was a classic hyperactive-hyperalert type. His behavior was ultimately seen—wrongly—as deriving from mania.

Like Indira, 16-year-old Dara was brought to the ER because of changes in mental status. Suddenly, he had become confused and began to "talk nonsense." Normally a quiet boy, he used profane language and spat at the nurses who attended to him. He was manageable only after being given Haldol. Dara then hyperventilated and became "rigid" and was transferred to Massachusetts General Hospital. His responses to most of the questions asked were minimal. He realized that he was in a hospital but did not know the day or the month.

Born in Cambodia, Dara had been in this country since he was an infant. He had never had a significant medical illness or any psychiatric illness and took no prescription medication. He had used marijuana in the past, but an extended toxicology screen in the ER was negative. After developing diarrhea, his mother had given him a Cambodian herbal tea. At some unspecified time later, his behavior became deranged.

While hospitalized, Dara experienced further episodes of muscle rigidity, which was relieved by Ativan. His creatine kinase (CK) level was 620 U/L (normal range, 60–320 U/L). Dara's confusion and disorientation continued. At no time did his temperature rise above 37.7 °C. With muscle rigidity and elevated CK levels, neuroleptic malignant syndrome (NMS) would have to be considered. However, the absence of fever and the rarity of this drug-induced neurological condition put NMS, at least initially, low on the list of possible explanations for Dara's symptoms.

On the second hospital day, the toxicology service identified strychnine in Dara's urine. Strychnine poisoning can cause both severe muscle rigidity and altered mental status. Some Cambodian herbal preparations are known to contain strychnine, and, because no other source of ingestion could be identified, it was concluded that Dara had been poisoned by strychnine in the herbal tea given to him by his mother!

Dara's stay in the hospital was longer than usual for patients with strychnine poisoning. The herbal product he had ingested contained diphenhydramine and chlorpheniramine, which were also found in his blood and urine. The anticholinergic effect of these antihistamines was thought to have reduced gastrointestinal motility and the absorption of strychnine—in effect, prolonging the poisoning.

While he was hospitalized, Dara's neuromuscular symptoms gradually resolved. Severe, prolonged muscle rigidity can cause rhabdomyolysis and myoglobinuria, which in turn can lead to renal failure. Despite having an elevated CK level, Dara did not develop this complication.

Dara was intermittently agitated, fearful, delusional, and disoriented. *Intermittently* is a key word here. According to the article from the Case Records of the Massachusetts General Hospital, "The administration of risperidone [Risperdal] resulted in partial improvement of his mental status. After an 11-day hospitalization, he was discharged with a concurrent diagnosis of psychosis. He is currently being seen by a psychiatrist.... His psychosis appears to be in remission, and he is functioning fairly well at home and in school."

Dara was discharged with the diagnoses of acute psychosis and bipolar disorder, along with strychnine poisoning. His medications were Risperdal, Ativan, Depakote, and Cogentin.

Dara had become a psychiatric patient!

In a letter to the editor of *The New England Journal of Medicine,* I explained why I felt that Dara's psychiatric diagnoses amounted to what Paul R. McHugh calls a "psychiatric misadventure." The letter was rejected, with the explanation that another letter, accepted for publication, expressed the same point of view. That letter, by C. J. Ryan and J. Anderson, appeared without a response from the authors of the original article.

It was argued in both letters that the diagnosis of delirium would have been sufficient to explain Dara's sudden and drastic changes in mental status. In the course of differentiating the diagnosis, the physicians attending him identified an "acute confusional state" (a more descriptive term for delirium used by somatic physicians), but neither acute confusional state nor delirium appeared in the discharge diagnosis. That delirium, which they recognized by another name, could be responsible for Dara's confusion, incoherent speech, uncharacteristic agitation and profanity, mood shifts, and psychosis was overlooked—even though the symptoms were described as intermittent, and intermittence is a hallmark of delirium.

Perhaps the time it took for Dara's delirium to clear even partially led his doctors to believe that another, psychiatric, cause had to be invoked—in spite of their plausible explanation that diphenhydramine and chlorpheniramine in the herbal tea Dara drank may have been responsible for the unusually long course of his muscle rigidity. Mental status changes accompanying delirium are known to resolve along with the delirium, though sometimes there is a lag between physiological correction and a full return to normal mental status. Some patients take longer than others to regain their emotional equilibrium.

Like depressed patients, manic patients sometimes have changes in behavior that make them appear delirious. However, manic patients do not have the clouded sensorium with severe cognitive impairment that is characteristic of delirium. Delirious patients are sometimes hyperactive and out of control, but they are not expansive and grandiose like patients with mania.

The *DSM-IV* makes it clear that bipolar disorder (or mania alone) may not be diagnosed until any suspected physiological factor is excluded as the cause of mood symptoms. Considering that Dara was still partially in the grip of delirium when he was discharged from the hospital, and that he had no history of mental illness, the diagnoses of bipolar disorder and acute psychosis should not have been made. Again, Slavney's observation is relevant: "As far as psychiatric disorders are concerned, delirium trumps everything."

Risperdal is sometimes used to control the symptoms of delirium that are most bothersome to patients and hospital staff. Perhaps Ativan alone would have been sufficient to hold Dara's agitation in check until the delirium ran its course. Prescribing Depakote here may have been unnecessary.

Consider this paradox: At a time when every deviation of thought, emotion, and behavior deemed worthy of being called a mental disorder is touted as having a physiological or genetic substrate, the myriad manifestations of delirium—the ultimate chemical imbalance of the brain—often go unrecognized.

Part V

How Patients' Stories Lead to a Psychiatric Diagnosis

Getting a patient's authentic story is essential to making a correct diagnosis, as well as an appropriate clinical intervention. But how can a clinical story be validated? If a patient's narrative reveals how self-deceiving choices have congealed into psychopathology—and after choosing a more authentic response the patient then experiences a surcease of pathological suffering and behavioral dysfunction—that narrative retrospectively takes on the face value of truth.

23

The Narrative in
Psychiatric Diagnosis
It's the Story, Stupid!

"Axioms in philosophy are not axioms until they are proven upon our pulses," wrote the poet John Keats, who was also a physician. At these moments, the beating heart seems to respond to what the brain knows with its own kind of understanding.

After working in the ER for eight years and evaluating more than 2000 patients, I have come to recognize the moment when the truth of a patient's situation reveals itself to me: I know what that person's life is up to. I know it in my head and in my gut. Sometimes, as happened with Dr. Keats, the epiphany quickens my pulse. That moment comes when the major elements of what I hear, see, and feel coalesce, so what was initially veiled and contradictory becomes clear and makes sense—I now have the patient's real story.

"Think horses, not zebras" is an axiom of medical diagnosis: it is the more common animal that we can expect to see more often. Driven by the inauthentic story, the tendency in psychiatry to overpathologize, overdiagnose, and overmedicate has generated many zebras, some of which find their way to the ER. Perhaps the worst consequence of these stories that turn troubled horses into even more troubled zebras is that the horses do not get a chance to discover and deal with the real problem.

After getting to a patient's authentic story in the ER, often after some struggle and unmasking, I am sometimes told the bogus story that led to the wrong diagnosis. Alice, a mildly mentally retarded 13-year-old girl, was one of the most dramatic and memorable of these exercises in unmasking. Alice was brought in by the police on emergency petition from her school. She had become agitated and had told the school nurse she was hearing voices and thinking of harming herself. Alice was in foster care and had been assigned a social worker by the Department of Social Services. This social worker had been called to the hospital and was with Alice when I entered the room to start the interview. I asked the social worker to wait in the lounge and assured her that we would confer after I spoke to the patient.

Whatever had agitated Alice earlier was not bothering her so much by the time I saw her. She was calm, engaging, and willing to talk. I do not recall all the details, but she had come from an abusive background and been placed with several different foster care families. Without hesitation, Alice told me that her latest crisis had started when she sensed that her foster mother's boyfriend did not want her around. She began to fear that her current custodial arrangement would end badly, as earlier ones had. Alice thought she was about to be "dumped" by her new family. Not knowing how to deal with this fear directly, she acted it out by becoming boisterous at school and telling the nurse that she was hearing voices and feeling suicidal.

Alice's paperwork from the Department of Social Services indicated that she had been diagnosed with schizoaffective disorder. She was taking an antipsychotic medication and a mood stabilizer. Before trying to understand the significance of the events that had brought Alice to the ER, I needed to find out how she came to be diagnosed as schizoaffective. First, I questioned her about auditory hallucinations, since she claimed to have heard voices earlier that day. I tried to determine if she could distinguish the voice of conscience, which is part of everyone's experience, particularly when stress becomes acute or when important things go wrong, from the kind of voice that is pathological (when your mind plays tricks on you) and is caused by an abnormal neural substrate. Without hesitation or embarrassment, Alice replied, "I never heard a voice. I never wanted to kill myself. I always say that when I don't get what I want." This was Alice's moment of truth. Perhaps she dropped the phony story because she was in the ER, or maybe because I had confronted her directly about the voices she claimed to hear. She assured me that she had never done anything to harm herself.

One might ask if the first clinician who took Alice's claim of auditory hallucinations at face value and made the schizoaffective diagnosis (which then became part of her psychiatric record) lacked an adequate degree of clinical skepticism and jumped to believe what Alice said. If Alice was telling me the truth, her story that had led to her diagnosis was false. The feigned auditory hallucinations undoubtedly figured heavily in that diagnosis. No other symptoms of a schizophrenia spectrum disorder were uncovered during my history-taking or were evident during the interview.

The nurse assigned to Alice asked me how, considering that Alice had lied before, I could be sure Alice was being truthful now. I answered that Alice had nothing to gain by lying to me and everything to gain by sticking to her original story about hearing voices and wanting to kill herself. In the past, this story had gotten her the attention of mental health clinicians, as well as several hospitalizations. She had been removed from tenuous or unsatisfactory living situations and was given greater bargaining power with the Department of Social Services, which becomes more solicitous when psychotic symptoms are part of the picture. I told the social worker about Alice's admitting that she had made up the voices and the threat to harm herself, and I asked her to pass on this information to the psychiatrist who prescribed Alice's medication.

Other patients I have seen in the ER received an incorrect diagnosis of schizophrenia or bipolar disorder not by deliberately deceiving a clinician, as Alice did, but by ultimately deceiving themselves. They thought they might be hearing voices (possibly because they heard about other patients' hearing voices), reported this to a mental health clinician, and had this claim accepted at face value. Then, after being given the diagnosis, they concluded that they *must* be having auditory hallucinations. They became convinced of this—falsely—with the complicity of the diagnostician. Their presumed sensory experience recalls how, in false memory syndrome, people cannot distinguish between an event that happened in their past from the *suggestion* that the event occurred, particularly when the reinforcement comes from an authority figure. These patients end up telling themselves and others induced stories, often to the detriment of everyone involved.

When evaluating a patient for auditory hallucinations, I start by saying, "You are hearing a voice now, and you know the voice you are hearing is my voice [many patients nod affirmatively here]. Have you ever heard a voice and not been sure who the speaker was?" I have found that these two sentences create a common ground that opens the way to diagnosing or ruling out auditory hallucinations. Many patients tell me they have heard their name called while walking down the street but could not identify the caller. Others say they heard voices or fragments of conversations while alone in a room. Questioned further, they acknowledge that these sounds may well have come from someone they did not see, or through the wall from an adjacent apartment. These reports do not suggest auditory hallucinations.

Many patients who are dependent on illicit drugs or alcohol, and who are destitute and homeless because of their addiction, come to the ER saying, "I am hearing voices, and I'm suicidal." They want to be admitted to the psychiatric unit so they can be fed and housed for a few days. "What are the voices saying?" I ask. The most common replies are "Hurt yourself"; "End it"; "Kill yourself"; "You're no good"; "You'll never amount to anything"; "You have no reason to be here"; "Go join your dead mother [or father, brother, sister]."

Most of these patients readily acknowledge that they have good reason to feel bad about themselves and put themselves down. Family members, spouses, and friends often have been strongly critical as well, some after having been abused and betrayed. I ask these patients how they can tell whether the "voice" they claim to hear is actually a voice or "is some part of you talking to yourself, like your conscience, which we all hear from time to time, or your memory of someone else criticizing you." (I apologize to the reader for breaking up the unitary self into metaphorical parts in the service of diagnosis.)

Many patients now begin to sense that I may be on to something. Their facial expression morphs to a look of knowing recognition, and sometimes of relief, possibly because they can now drop the pretense of being psychotic. "Maybe that's it" is a common reply—words that ring true to me. "It's probably not really a voice." The majority of patients who initially report this kind of voice deny they have heard voices giving other commands or making other comments. How likely is it that someone who is homeless and positive for cocaine or heroin will have auditory hallucinations limited to these deprecating commands? Most patients acknowledge as much by the end of the interview and agree that they need to stop using drugs, find a place to live, and try to make amends to the people they have hurt through their addiction.

With this point clarified, the clinician must still determine if a patient's nonpsychotic internal "voice," which may be a component of his or her real story, represents a significant threat of self-harm. One does not need to have command hallucinations to be genuinely suicidal.

After evaluating more than 2000 patients in the ER, I have seen perhaps 15 who I believed were really hearing voices, and about half of them denied it. I inferred their psychosis either from direct observation of an apparent response to internal stimuli, or I took the word of a clinician or family member who offered what seemed to be incontrovertible evidence. These were mainly patients who were truly bipolar or schizophrenic and were off their medication or were experiencing an increase in stress. A few were patients with severe depression. You can say that their voices were felt in my gut and "proven" on my pulse.

It is crucial to determine if a patient's report of "hearing voices" represents a true psychotic experience. The call on this issue will divide that person's world in half. Depending on which half a patient is assigned to—and resides in—he or she will have a different self-understanding, response from others, diagnosis, treatment, and, quite likely, outcome. Clinicians who encourage patients to believe they are having psychotic experiences when this is not the case can do significant harm.

A clinician who is listening to a patient's story, and is trying to go from there to a diagnosis, would do well to keep in mind the dictum of

William of Ockham, a 14th-century scholastic philosopher, that still influences modern thought. This is "Ockham's razor," also known as the
principle of parsimony: when there are multiple ways to explain a phenomenon, go with the one that requires the fewest—or least drastic—
assumptions. Listen for the elaborations that patients spin out on their
stories that do not quite ring true. Challenge these productions. If true,
the stories will stand up to scrutiny. Most patients understand and respect this kind of persistence. Of course, some will resent the intrusion
on their efforts to deceive you and themselves. Ultimately, they will not
be helped by your buying their lies.

When you suspect a patient's previous diagnosis may be wrong,
try to imagine the patient's deliberate lie or self-deception, and the
subsequent elaboration of the story, that may have led an unsuspecting
clinician to erroneously diagnose a mental disorder. Ask yourself if a
lesser diagnosis could account for the facts as they emerge after the
subtext (real story) is uncovered. Let Ockham's razor cut away the dis-
torting elaboration.

"Think horses, not zebras" is an axiom of medical diagnosis: it is
the more common animal that we can expect to see more often. Driven
by the inauthentic story, the tendency in psychiatry to overpathologize,
overdiagnose, and overmedicate has generated many zebras, some of
which find their way to the ER. Perhaps the worst consequence of
these stories that turn troubled horses into even more troubled zebras
is that the horses do not get a chance to discover and deal with the real
problem.

This point is solidly made by the story of a patient I saw in private
practice. Tina, a woman in her late 40s, came to the group I practiced
with after her insurance would no longer pay for her to see the psychiatrist whom she had worked with for more than 10 years. This psychiatrist
had diagnosed Tina with bipolar disorder (manic depression) and kept
her on lithium for a decade. It soon became evident that Tina was classi-
cally histrionic; she easily met the *DSM-IV* criteria for histrionic personality disorder. Not only did she never have a manic episode during the 10
years she took lithium, but she had never been hypomanic—just floridly

histrionic. Tina's highest highs and lowest lows did not even meet the criteria for bipolar II disorder.

A psychiatrist colleague determined to his own satisfaction that Tina had been wrongly diagnosed with bipolar disorder, and he tapered her off the lithium. Tina did not become manic or hypomanic, nor did she become more depressed, though she was more anxious. For more than a decade, Tina had taken her psychiatrist's word that her "mood swings" were caused by a chemical imbalance that she could do nothing about, except take lithium. Patients with personality disorders, particularly histrionic and borderline personality structures, are going to have mood swings, sometimes dramatic ones. If a patient's story and dynamics suggest such a personality structure, that is the primary problem to be addressed. Trying to treat these dynamics solely by diagnosing and medicating a primary mood disorder completely misses the point.

I saw Tina weekly for therapy. She was bright and was willing to acknowledge the self-deception that had forged her histrionic defenses against the childhood and adolescent pressures she had faced. After about two months of therapy, the anxiety that had grown out of her weakened defenses became harder for her to manage. In spite of my trying not to be judgmental as we uncovered the meaning of her life story, she felt guilty about the considerable pain she had caused her husband and daughter in the name of a chemical imbalance. After thanking me for what I had done for her (sincerely, I believe), she fired me, saying she planned to work with someone else.

If an accurate psychiatric diagnosis is to be made for Tina or for any patient, the story told has to be stripped of its uniqueness and reduced to its most significant narrative elements. This distillate can then be matched to the reductions that the clinical science of psychiatry (now largely the *DSM-IV*) has made from the distillates of patients' stories already listened to and diagnosed. If you shortchange either the story or the clinical science, you lose the truth about what the patient's life is up to. An analogy from the neurophysiology of vision illustrates this point: both eyes, with nerve fibers crossing at the optic chiasm, are required for a full visual field; a lesion along the optic track for either eye results in a field cut that distorts vision. Miss a patient's real story, or fail to identify the tenets of clinical psychiatry relevant to it, and you get what amounts to a field cut in the diagnosis and treatment.

If a clinician does not get a patient's story right, nothing that follows from the wrong story will be right either: not the diagnosis, not the medication prescribed, and not the psychotherapy. To paraphrase the directive that was so instrumental in getting Bill Clinton elected to his first presidential term—It's the story, stupid! These words are intended to provoke awareness, not to insult. Whenever I work with a patient, I try to heed this clarion call. Getting the story right is the first step in ensuring that the uniqueness of the patient is not lost to abstractions, generalities, or deliberate fabrications.

Alexithymia
When There Is No Story to Tell

Once the distortions are cleared away, most patients who come to the ER tell stories that seem to have grown out of the problems they claim to have and the pain they claim to feel. These stories reverberate with emotions congruent with the themes of the story. But occasionally patients who do have problems and are in great emotional pain tell incongruent stories. They will insist that they have no problems, that their life is fine, and that they have no idea what is wrong. Their story is that they have no story. These patients cannot find the words to describe their feelings.

Identifying a patient as alexithymic opens a door to that person's pathological world and creates a fertile field for exploration in therapy. A workable identity can develop only after the elements of a person's life coalesce into a minimally satisfactory story.

In 1972, Peter Sifneos introduced to psychiatry the term *alexithymia*. Derived from the Greek, the word literally means "having no words for emotions" (*a* = lack, *lexis* = word, *thymos* = emotions). Alexithymia is not a diagnosis, but a construct useful for understanding patients who seem not to understand the feelings they experience and who lack the words to describe those feelings to others. Identifying this deficit in expressivity is important because doing so gives the clinician a leg up in making a diagnosis and charting a therapeutic course.

Many persons with alexithymia have somatic complaints. There is a good deal of empirical evidence linking prolonged states of emotional arousal, and the complementary physiological arousal, with susceptibility to certain somatic disorders. Someone who cannot verbally express negative emotions has trouble discharging and neutralizing these emotions, physiologically as well as psychically. All feelings, whether normal or pathological, are ultimately bodily feelings. People with alexithymia lack an understanding of what they experience emotionally. The concept of alexithymia overlaps with that of "masked depression," often described as depression hidden by (and possibly "converted" to) somatic symptoms or manifested as aberrant behavior.

From the perspective of development, alexithymia implies a glitch in the process that permits the expression of feelings in words that capture the body's involvement in these feelings. Perhaps the child's mother failed to sufficiently encourage a language of feelings (which would surely exclude her from the pantheon of Winnicott's "good-enough" mothers). Alternatively, emotional trauma later in life may compromise the connection between what is felt and what can be grasped about this feeling and put into words, particularly if the link was tenuous to begin with.

If a patient has no story to tell a clinician, even when emotions are stirred high enough to prompt an ER visit, it seems a good bet that the person has no story to tell himself either. Having no story almost certainly implies an impaired identity: who we know ourselves to be depends heavily on the story we tell ourselves about who we are. The inability to express emotions verbally implies a deficient interior life. Inevitably, those who cannot match words to feelings will live out that deficit in their contacts with others as well. To have no words for one's inner experience is to live marginally, for oneself and for others.

Kisha, 16, was brought to the ER by her mother after she held a curling iron to the outside of her left upper arm, causing a large, painful burn. Kisha had just started her junior year in high school and also worked as a cashier in a convenience store. She was an average student, but her mother assured me she was one of the most popular girls in her class. Kisha lived with her parents, two sisters, and a brother. She had never used illicit drugs or abused alcohol. "I'm a virgin," she said easily and proudly when I asked if she had a current boyfriend, which she did not. Kisha denied physical and sexual abuse, and her mother later corroborated her denial. Asthma, occasional bronchitis, and seasonal allergies were her only concessions to good health.

Asked how she felt during the interview, Kisha answered with an easy smile, "I feel fine." It seemed to me that her happy face owed more to practice than to spontaneity. I doubted that her affect reflected her mood, either then or earlier that day. When I asked Kisha why she had burned herself so seriously, she looked at me blankly and said she did not know. She denied that anything had changed in her life recently. She acknowledged no disappointment or setback, no problems at home or at school. According to Kisha, everything was fine.

The burn that brought Kisha to the ER the evening I interviewed her was not her first act of self-mutilation. Seven months earlier, she had jumped out of a second-story window. Inexplicably, she did not go to a hospital, for either medical treatment or psychiatric evaluation. I was the first mental health clinician Kisha had spoken to. During the previous year, Kisha also had made modest cuts with a razor on the underside of one forearm and on her cheek—"I was just bored" was her explanation. Asked why she jumped out of the window, her only response was "I have no idea." She denied that this potentially lethal act had anything to do with what was going on in her life at the time. Despite my persistent efforts to elicit more information about the reason for Kisha's self-destructive behavior, she did not offer a scintilla of explanation. That she could find no reasons for what she had done did not strike her as the least bit odd.

Kisha's mother told me, with understatement, that her daughter "keeps it all inside." Apparently, Kisha was not the only minimizer in this family. The mother also volunteered that Kisha had trouble getting over disappointments. The day before she burned herself with the curling iron, a woman who had promised to take Kisha to a museum in another city abruptly canceled the trip. At the time she jumped from the window, Kisha was having problems with a boyfriend, and the relationship ended soon after. Kisha vigorously denied she had difficulty getting over disappointments in general, or that a particular disappointment had anything to do with any of her self-destructive acts. Her mother thought differently. Kisha had no words for the feelings that led her to do these things. But her silence spoke volumes. Clearly, she had emotions she did not acknowledge or understand. This young woman put a smile on her despair and gave no hint of what was going on under the mask.

Most patients who come to the ER after harming themselves are eager to discuss the meaning of what they did. Complex issues are explored, often with startling insight. These patients are willing to have their initial, often self-deceiving explanations challenged and to allow the subtext of their destructive acts to be interpreted to them. But after Kisha burned her arm, no words came to name the emotions that had driven her to do this. She clarified nothing, for herself or for me. Kisha was alexithymic.

Among the many self-mutilating patients I have evaluated in the ER, the most memorable was an attractive 19-year-old college student who had cut marks of various lengths and depths all over her arms, legs, and torso. The incision that brought her to the ER was made with a razor blade on the underside of her right wrist. After the initial incision, several cuts went deeper than she intended, and a tendon was severed. The hand surgeon who was called in the middle of the night to do the repair had trouble locating the proximal end of the tendon, which had retracted into the forearm after snapping. While he called his supervisor for assistance, I did my interview.

This young woman, lying on a gurney under bright fluorescent lights and facing a long period of rehabilitation with an uncertain outcome, unabashedly told me about the problems she had, her feelings of anxiety and depression, and how for many years she had tried to counter this emotional pain by cutting her body and watching the blood come.

Many patients who mutilate themselves as Kisha did have borderline personality disorder. During the interview, and later in a separate conversation with Kisha's mother, I looked hard for borderline dynamics and symptoms. Besides Kisha's obvious, though unacknowledged, proclivity for turning disappointment into physical self-injury, I could not identify any. In spite of her denying the cardinal symptoms of major depression,

I had little doubt that Kisha was in fact experiencing depression, with what the *DSM-IV* calls atypical features. Reading the subtext of her nonstory, I felt I could infer the symptoms she denied.

Kisha told me she did not have any further intention or plan to harm herself. I believed that was true for the moment, but, at the same time, I felt that she was not finished with these self-destructive acts. Kisha did not need to be hospitalized. She did need immediate, intensive outpatient therapy with someone who knew how to draw her out and help her put words to the feelings—whatever they were, wherever they came from—that were eating at her from the inside and causing her to mutilate herself on the outside.

Maureen, 37, was brought to the ER by her parents. "I've been very depressed," she said when I asked why she had come. The day before, Maureen had gone to another ER, specifically, she told me, "to get a different antidepressant." She was taking Prozac, prescribed by a general practitioner two years earlier, with little or no benefit. Denied a new medication in the ER, she became, by her own account, "hysterical" and "ran out" without discharge instructions.

"I feel like I have hit rock bottom," Maureen told me. "I cry all the time. I feel like I have no control over myself." She had been seen by two psychiatrists briefly 15 years earlier but had no treatment since, in spite of periodic recurrences of her depression. "I feel as depressed now as ever," she said. "I have no hope of getting better." The depression had become worse through the preceding three months. During that time, her sleep had increased from seven to 10 hours a night. Her appetite increased somewhat, and she had gained five pounds. She appeared slightly overweight.

Maureen had completed two years of college and now worked as a photographer for a company that supplied photos of sports events for high school and college yearbooks. Her job was competitive and stressful. At certain times of the year she worked up to 80 hours a week, often facing tight deadlines. "I put more pressure on myself than the job does," she said with no apparent regret. In spite of her increasing depression during the past three months, Maureen's boss was satisfied with her work, though Maureen did not feel she was performing well. Everything required more effort now. It was harder to concentrate. Maureen found what she did less interesting, and she cut back her social activities considerably. She got little joy from work and contact with friends. Losing her edge made her feel guilty.

Maureen was unquestionably having an episode of major depression. From her story and the fact she had been on Prozac for two years, an underlying dysthymic disorder was also likely, giving her what the *DSM-IV* calls "double depression." She also experienced a good deal of anxiety and was prescribed Klonopin, as needed. Maureen denied ever using illicit drugs or abusing alcohol.

Maureen insisted she had no intention or plan to harm herself but added, "I can't imagine living my life this way indefinitely." Fifteen years earlier, she had "tried to get up the nerve to take a bottle of pills," but could not. Five years earlier, she had sat in her car with the motor running and the garage door shut for five minutes but terminated this potentially lethal act because, she told me, she "couldn't go through with it."

When I asked Maureen why she thought she was feeling depressed, she did not acknowledge a single negative factor in her life (though unlike Kisha, she did at least admit to having symptoms of depression). Questioning her about her marriage, job, finances, and family produced no revelations. She had supportive parents, a relatively secure if stressful job she liked and excelled at, and no financial problems. She had been married for about 15 years, had no children, and thought of her relationship with her husband as good.

Asked how she and her husband related sexually, Maureen told me with no apparent regret that her partner was impotent and that they had had sex only a few times during their marriage, though they still shared some lesser intimacies. How did Maureen feel about this lack of sex in her life? "I got used to it," she said nonchalantly. She insisted she was "very happy" in her marriage and had no complaints about her husband.

Maureen readily volunteered that her first sexual experience had occurred at age 15 and that she had had six or seven sexual partners before marrying. She reported these facts almost clinically, as if speaking about someone else. She told me this while sitting upright on a gurney and wearing tan, cuffed shorts, bare legs un–self-consciously displayed, making good eye contact, and talking in a pleasant, round tone. I was not convinced that Maureen had made as good an accommodation to living a sexless life as she would have herself and me believe.

I regret not asking Maureen if she had been involved with another man (or woman) during her 15-year marriage, if she had wanted to be involved, or if she had ever been frustrated in her efforts to be involved. Her answers could have given some hint of what was underneath a story that had no words for feelings so painful that she was at "rock bottom," saw no hope of feeling better, and had gone to two different ERs in two days.

Maureen was taking Fioricet for severe headaches, which her doctor told her were not migraines. She also had abdominal pain. Several years earlier, she had had a total hysterectomy for endometriosis, and she was on Premarin. Hoping to get a better sense of how much pain Maureen's body caused her, I asked her to rate that pain on a scale of one to six (the somatic concern item on the Brief Psychiatric Rating Scale). Quickly, she answered four. If Maureen had no words for her emotional pain, at least she could be quantitative about her physical pain! Perhaps she was one of those alexithymic patients who had somatic symptoms related to her inability to discharge negative emotions and neutralize the physiological concomitants of prolonged emotional arousal. (Kisha, on the other hand, acknowledged only those somatic symptoms related to the physical injuries she inflicted on her body.)

Maureen was in considerable emotional distress, but did not need to be hospitalized. I referred her to a psychiatrist who was committed to doing intensive outpatient psychotherapy.

Though it is not fully validated empirically, alexithymia is a useful clinical construct. For Kisha and Maureen, this word, so descriptive in its Greek roots, specifies a real phenomenon and identifies a deficit of self. Neither woman shut down or clammed up only for her ER interview. The disconnect between feeling and words was part and parcel of the

daily experience of both women. They were attractive, personable, out-
going, and articulate—except about their feelings. Neither showed any
sign of schizoid personality disorder, a diagnosis that needs to be considered when patients seem detached from their feelings and lack insight.
Being able to say that Kisha and Maureen had no words for their feelings
was a major first step in identifying what was pathological about their
worlds. How could anyone who could not discharge negative emotions
over many years *not* be depressed or have any number of other emotional
and somatic problems?

Identifying a patient as alexithymic opens a door to that person's
pathological world and creates a fertile field for exploration in therapy.
A workable identity can develop only after the elements of a person's life
coalesce into a minimally satisfactory story. To paraphrase Winnicott, a
"good-enough" identity requires a "good-enough" story. It is the therapist's job to help the alexithymic patient convert a nonstory into a story
that is at least partially authentic, so that a more authentic identity can
evolve from that story.

25   Renegotiating the "Contract for Safety"

The most critical call anyone evaluating patients in the ER will make is whether patients are at risk for taking their own lives or the lives of others. This is known as the issue of safety, and some clinicians believe that an adequate safety assessment should involve a contract proscribing this behavior. After hearing the patient's version of events up to that time, a clinician assessing his or her safety is being asked to make a judgment about part of a life-story that is yet to be lived. From my own experience, and from what I learned from others who do this work, I gradually came to question—and then reject—the value of such a contract struck with an ER patient.

At times, I do not know in my head or in my gut why a patient took an overdose or chose some other act of self-harm. Sometimes, I sense that a patient may not have exhausted the need to act out a conflict in a harmful way. I hospitalize these patients, regardless of what they contract for.

"Will the patient contract for safety?" a clinician or insurance representative at the other end of the line wants to know. "I don't know," I answer. Often I will add, "And I don't care." I then explain why I believe that an ER "contract for safety" is clinically unsound and can, for some patients, lead to disaster.

"I want out," a despondent Julia told her primary-care physician in his office. Along with hypertension, fluid retention, glaucoma, and asthma, this 36-year-old woman had been treated for depression during the last year. Concerned about her safety after hearing this apparent cry from the depths, the doctor drove her to the ER. "I want out," Julia told the triage nurse during the initial medical evaluation. When I entered her room, Julia was lying quietly on a gurney. Her mother and father, looking

175

grave, sat in chairs. I needed to talk to Julia alone and suggested to the parents that they go to the waiting room.

Julia was not married, did not have children, and lived with her parents. She worked as a nurse-technician at a nearby hospital. Julia had been feeling well until a year before, when her 89-year-old grandfather died. After his death, she was overwhelmed with grief and became depressed. Her primary-care physician started her on Prozac, which was titrated to 40 mg. The drug calmed her down at first but then seemed to lose its efficacy. Julia's doctor told her that she had a "disease." She did not see a psychotherapist.

One month before coming to the ER, Julia's 89-year-old grandmother died. With this second death of a close family member in less than a year, Julia's depression became more severe. She began to lose the sense of who she was. Her Prozac was increased to 60 mg but without apparent effect. In some way Julia could not specify, she began to feel "unsafe." Julia continued working but found it hard to concentrate. She felt under constant stress, had interrupted sleep and was tired during the day. She "ate everything in sight," gained weight, had little interest in doing many of the things she normally did, and associated only with family members and coworkers.

Fifteen years earlier, Julia had been depressed and saw a psychotherapist for six months. She could not recall what was going on in her life at that time that might have predisposed her to depression. Julia did not drink alcohol or use illicit drugs. She was taking medication for asthma and hypertension, which were well controlled.

Julia was immediately and fully responsive to the questions I asked. Though occasionally tearful, she seemed happy to be talking to someone. She was obviously frightened about her situation and was trying hard to rein in her emotions. Julia was not sure what was happening to her, and it soon became evident that the anxiety associated with this confusion was the acute component of her year-long mood disturbance. I was surprised when Julia let it be known, almost incidentally, that she felt guilty about her grandfather's death. She was the last person to see him before he died, and a cousin was miffed that

Julia had not contacted her so that she, too, could have been present. That Julia could be made to feel guilty for such an "infraction," particularly considering how much time she had spent with each grandparent during their final illnesses, shows how psychologically vulnerable this woman was. The guilt her cousin put on her was clearly a factor in this case of complicated bereavement.

I reminded Julia that living to age 89 is a privilege given to few. As I said this, a part of her burden seemed to lift. Her affect brightened through the interview, and she was smiling near the end. She told me she was grateful that I was talking to her about her grandparents and how she felt about them. I explained that Prozac might calm her down, and maybe give her a "boost," but that it could not resolve the issues created by her loss or neutralize the guilt she was feeling.

I still had to find out what Julia meant when she said, "I want out"—the statement that had gotten her to the ER and set the stage for our interview. At first, Julia said she did not know what these words meant, and she acknowledged being confused and overwhelmed by her feelings. I asked if, during the last month, as her depression deepened, she had ever thought of doing anything specific that would threaten her life. No, she said, emphatically. She denied ever trying to harm herself in the past. So what did Julia mean by wanting "out?" What did she want "out" of? Not life itself, apparently. Like so many patients I have evaluated in the ER who said "I want out" and "I don't want to be here anymore," I believe Julia wanted "out" of the intense emotional pain that guilt and depression were causing her. Julia was confused and hurting, but she was not hopeless and despairing. We came to a shared understanding that she was not likely to harm herself.

Before discharging her from the ER, I needed to know how Julia saw herself getting through the next few days. She was anticipating a restless night or two, with some floor-walking to offset her nervous energy. Julia wanted a week off from work, away from the stress of her job. "I need someone to talk to," she said with conviction. "You have been very helpful." I took her words to mean that she had come to recognize implicitly a psychodynamic reason for her pain, as well as the need for psychotherapy. Just to get her reaction, I asked Julia if she felt that a hospitalization would help her. No, she said, citing among other reasons her reluctance to be confined to a small space, like a hospital room. I was convinced that she would not benefit from being admitted and that this kind of sequestration most likely would impede her recovery. Her parents felt that it was safe for her to go home. Her father agreed to take a few days off from work to be with her.

I have helped hundreds of ER patients acknowledge the reason for their self-injurious gestures. Typically, someone who has just had a messy confrontation with a parent, spouse, or significant other will take a number of pills. These pills may be the patient's prescribed medication, someone else's prescribed medication, or an over-the-counter medication. Some patients call 911 themselves. Others tell someone else about what they have done, and that person calls 911 or brings the patient to the hospital. Once a patient is in the ER, the poison control center is contacted and given the specifics of the overdose. Pharmacology experts there make recommendations for treatment based on protocols. After the patient has been medically cleared, someone from the psychiatry service is called in to do an evaluation.

In all but a handful of overdose cases, I have been able to work with the patient to understand what led to the overdose. Most patients reveal their intention quickly and gladly. "I wanted attention" is the most common reason given. Others admit they were trying to punish a family member or significant other who they felt had wronged them. Typically, someone who was not getting his or her way and was not willing to take an instrumental next step to resolve the underlying conflict decided to dramatize the point. Countless mothers (and not a few fathers), reflecting on the situation, have told me that their adolescent son or daughter had just "thrown a pity party." What some patients try to say with pills, others express with superficial cuts, usually to the ventral wrist.

Patients love to talk about why they make these gestures. It is as if they have finally been listened to and understood. They are now getting the attention they have craved for so long. This success justifies to them the need for having spoken in the code of gestural self-harm. Many feel that the discomfort of a nasogastric tube and charcoal lavage, or the sight of the bloody wrist, was worth it, though most also say they will not try this again. They leave the ER believing they have accomplished something, and in a sense they have. I try to get them to acknowledge that there are better ways to be heard and to get the kind of attention they should be seeking. When I see patients absorbing this point, I feel that my time with them was well spent.

Some patients come to the ER down on their luck because of their bad behavior, which often involves substance abuse and the betrayal of everyone they know because of it. They have no money and no place to stay. These patients often make a point of *not* contracting for safety. "I'm suicidal," they will tell the triage nurse. Some add, "I'm also homicidal," presumably hoping to cover all the bases in their bid for a hospital bed. There is that old ER saying, "The patient knew what to say"—that is, knew what to tell the ER staff to get admitted and receive the proverbial "three hots and a cot."

Clinicians who evaluate psychiatric patients in the ER should be able to determine what patients who "know what to say" really mean. After interviewing several hundred ER patients, many of them substance abusers, I began to feel what I can only describe as a new degree of confidence in making a determination about a patient's safety. (Surgeons call this blending of discipline and instinct *unconscious competence*.) Clinicians just honing their skills will wish, as the saying goes, to err on the side of caution. At the same time, we need to learn how not to be manipulated by those who would use mental health facilities to reduce the consequences of their bad behavior. One patient who was broke and homeless, who I was certain was no threat to himself or others, insisted, "I'm so suicidal I'll never make it home." Another patient told me, "I'm so suicidal I'll never make it out of the ER." I discharged both.

At times, I do not know in my head or in my gut why a patient took an overdose or chose some other act of self-harm. Sometimes, I sense that a patient may not have exhausted the need to act out a conflict in a harmful way. I hospitalize these patients, regardless of what they contract for. Ultimately, I try to determine whether a patient can imagine a future in spite of the difficulties, and has the will and the capacity to deal with what is ahead. True despair, the kind that drives the real suicidal act, is the lack of this will and capacity.

I did not ask Julia to contract for safety as a condition for discharge from the ER. I have come to see these contracts, made in the heat of crisis with a clinician who the patient does not know, as intrinsically unreliable and essentially different from the agreement often made in outpatient therapy. Outpatient contracts that are struck with a clinician when a therapeutic alliance is already established have proven effective in containing the self-destructive impulses of suicidal patients.

Like patients who have no other place to go and "know what to say" to be admitted, patients who have already made up their minds to do serious harm to themselves or others also "know what to say" to be discharged from the ER. One patient's ER contract for safety, apparently accepted at face value, led to a tragedy. I know the story only secondhand, but the source is a reliable one. A woman in her 30s was brought by her brother to the ER of another hospital. Two facts dominated the case: (1) at home, the depressed woman had threatened to kill herself; and (2) the brother's gun was missing, and he was sure the patient had taken it. A social worker was called in to do an evaluation and make a determination. The patient vehemently denied having any intention or plan to harm herself and denied that she had taken her brother's gun. She wanted to be discharged. A verbal contract for safety was made with the social worker.

The patient's brother was certain that her threat earlier that day to harm herself was real, and he demanded that she be certified. Believing the patient's claim made in the ER that she was not suicidal, the social worker discharged her. Several days later, the patient drove to a neighboring state, checked into a motel, and shot herself to death. The family sued the hospital. I do not wish to second-guess the social worker's clinical evaluation, though I wonder if the brother's missing gun would have triggered my suspicion of the patient's suicidal intention and plan. I do not know all that went into the decision to discharge this woman from the ER, but I suspect that her contract for safety figured significantly.

At a time when psychiatry is trying to explain most mental illness by positing a glitch in brain chemistry—the iconic "chemical imbalance"—it seems both perverse and refreshing to reach across to the opposite pole of human knowledge in the hope of understanding at least some of the mind's derangements. By showing us how choice is a fundamental component of all human experience—and how a choice made in self-deception, the lie we tell ourselves, distorts our Being—the philosopher Jean-Paul Sartre has given us a powerful tool for understanding mental illness, along with an implied therapeutic. Much of Sartre's ontology is felt, if indirectly, in what is probably the most successful psychotherapeutic technique used now, cognitive therapy, developed by the psychiatrist Aaron Beck.

Ultimately, we all choose what is tolerable or intolerable for us. According to Sartre, the only thing we cannot choose is not to choose, even if that choice is made by default. We are, he said, "condemned to freedom." This is our anguish, as well as our glory.

Aside from those with schizophrenia, bipolar disorder, or dementia, many of the patients I evaluate in the ER have problems that become transparent when vetted with this sound bite from Jean-Paul Sartre: "I regard mental illness as the 'way out' that the free organism, in its total unity, invents in order to be able to live through an intolerable situation."

Sartre was one of a group of European philosophers who broke with the dominant Western Cartesian dualism to create a new philosophy, which came to be known as existentialism. This approach to understanding human behavior eventually spawned the discipline of existential psychiatry. The leading figures in this movement include Ludwig Binswanger, Medard Boss, Erwin Straus, Viktor Frankl, Karl Jaspers, R. D. Laing, and J. H. van den Berg. In North America, the psychiatrist Irving Yalom and the psychologist Rollo May were among those strongly influenced by existential theory.

To Sartre, the fundamental fact about our existence is that it is free; we make it up as we go along, rather than live out an essence that is given to us more or less ready-made. "Existence precedes essence" is Sartre's famous formulation of his concept of freedom. To maintain, contrary to Sartre, that essence precedes existence is to allot a lesser role to freedom in understanding how our lives are made. The essences that are considered to be the principal driving forces behind human existence include the unconscious, genetics, neurochemistry, and a Supreme Being.

Sartre saw mental illness as a perturbation of human existence that can occur when persons use their freedom to make self-deceiving choices—choices that give primacy to essence over existence. Paradoxically, this use of freedom—really a misuse—that involves a betrayal of the self and its authentic possibilities, makes one unfree in a painful and debilitating way. "Painfully unfree" is a good way to characterize how life seems to those who are mentally ill. Sartre first posited freedom as an absolute. Later, he conceded that other factors can influence and limit the person one ultimately becomes. Even with Sartre's own qualification, his insistence on the role of free will in precipitating mental illness is strong, esoteric stuff that happens to play out remarkably well in the ER. With Sartre at my side, I have listened to hundreds of patients tell the story of how self-deceiving choices, featuring a "way out" of an "intolerable situation," eventually compromised their lives.

One story came from Chris, a 15-year-old boy who was brought to the ER by his family. While arguing with his father, Chris had reached for a knife. He had been hospitalized for eight days during the previous month after threatening to harm himself. Chris had made similar threats before but had never acted on them. Chris was diagnosed with oppositional-defiant disorder and attention deficit disorder in the second grade; in the fifth grade, he was diagnosed with major depressive disorder. Chris was taking Effexor, Neurontin, and Concerta. He saw a social worker weekly for three and a half years but had recently stopped. "That did not end as it should have," his father told me, offering no further explanation.

This young man was 50 pounds overweight and flabby. His serum glucose level was 149 mg/dL, indicating a mild hyperglycemia consistent with physical inactivity and obesity. He had lost a significant amount of hair from his head, a condition his primary-care physician diagnosed as stress alopecia. Chris denied ever using recreational drugs or drinking alcohol. His toxicology screen was negative.

Knowing that Chris had the oppositional-defiant diagnosis and had just threatened his father, I was prepared to meet an angry, defiant adolescent. Instead, I found myself taking to a polite, cooperative young man who seemed to have as much insight into his life as he had trouble living it. It soon became evident that Chris had no intention of harming himself or anyone else. "I went for the knife to get my father to take me seriously," he told me, immediately and un–self-consciously. This acknowledgment was my entry point into Chris's disordered world.

Chris was not getting along with his parents, who were divorced. He admitted that he had deliberately not put any serious effort into his academic work or sports. "If I fail," he told me, "things will be worse than they are now." This is classic self-handicapping. Chris's fear of failing almost certainly contributed to the chip he carried so prominently on his shoulder. The related attitude he displayed at home and at school (but not during our interview) had gotten him into a good deal of trouble with his parents and school officials.

Chris's father was a hard-driving, successful accountant. He had played football in college and had a $30,000 gym in his basement. Chris lived with his mother, a social worker, who was herself seeing a therapist for depression and was taking antidepressant medication. His maternal aunt and several others on his mother's side of the family were also being treated for depression. Chris's father had remarried. He insisted that he had moved on with his life after the divorce but that his ex-wife, who was still single, had not.

During our interview, Chris made it clear that he had never realized that he had a choice about the person he could become. Seeing his failure and unhappiness as inevitable, he quickly cited two reasons for this determinism: genetics and God. He felt that, because his mother and other family members were depressed, his life was already cast by his DNA, which had created a chemical imbalance in his brain. Why Chris believed that a Supreme Being had such a limited plan for him he never said. This was Chris's "way out" of his difficult family dynamic, the "intolerable situation" he ultimately chose not to overcome. Chris, in effect, had convinced himself that his essence preceded his existence, pathologically perturbing that existence in the process.

Chris acknowledged that fear had kept him from putting himself on the line and taking the risks required to accomplish what most boys his age would normally go for. Fear was also undoubtedly behind the indirect, metaphorical way he communicated his feelings of powerlessness and frustration to his parents, teachers, and friends. This style has worked strongly against him. When I asked Chris what impression he felt he had made on the teachers and administrators at his middle school, he unabashedly responded that he was seen as being "suicidal and violent." How had he given that impression? Chris acknowledged that, since the sixth grade, whenever he was feeling particularly frustrated and powerless, he would tell those around him, "I feel like killing myself." Asked what he was trying to signify with these words, he responded, "I want help. I don't want to feel that way." Chris convinced me that he had never actually wanted to harm himself or had a plan to do so.

Chris's style of communicating with his parents and peers led school officials and counselors to be concerned that, besides being a threat to himself, Chris might also want to harm others. Miscommunication bred of frustration drove Chris to use hyperbolic words and phrases that were heard as threats by administrators who had a post-Columbine sensitivity. As I was probing for the potential of violence, Chris convincingly told me, "I'm not violent. I'm either the one being punched or the one running away." Chris denied ever having had any intention or plan to harm anyone. When he got into jams at school, his pattern was to "mouth off and leave." His behavior was maladaptive but not dangerous. Chris made it clear that he did not harbor any resentment against any of the students, teachers, or administrators at his school. In fact, he felt that he wasn't treated all that badly there considering how he acted (again, his good, if selective, insight). The only threat I saw for Chris was that, without significantly changing his stance toward the world, he would continue to waste his life. I believe that the mental health profession and the school system both got Chris wrong. By not understanding what his life was all about, they missed their chance to help him.

Two months after I saw Chris in the ER, his father called to ask me to write an evaluation supporting Chris's application to a military preparatory school. The program there was geared to students with academic and disciplinary problems. I met with Chris for two hours. He was still taking Effexor and Neurontin, but not Concerta, which had been prescribed to improve his concentration during the school term. There had been no other significant incidents at home and no other ER visits.

Trying to understand the difficulties that Chris had had for so many years, I first considered the possibility that his problems may have been rooted in a personality disorder. I probed for pervasive patterns of behavior in the dysfunction that marked his life. Nothing I heard from Chris or his parents, or read in the evaluations from his social worker and a school psychologist that his father passed on to me, suggested this kind of mental disorder. Even the oppositional-defiant diagnosis seemed shaky when weighed against the fact that Chris kept his weekly appointments with a therapist for more than three years, took the medication his psychiatrist prescribed, and was polite, courteous, and especially forthcoming during our interviews. What was Chris opposing? Who was he defying?

I then looked into whether a primary mood disorder could have dogged Chris's efforts to succeed. He had been diagnosed with major depression in the fifth grade and was still taking medication for depression.

Meeting him for the first time when he was in the eighth grade, I cannot say how depressed he may have been earlier. At the time of the ER interview, a month after an eight-day inpatient hospitalization precipitated by a suicide threat, and during the two hours I spent with him two months later, his mood seemed more like dysthymia than like major depression. His father told me that Chris always felt better when he left his mother's house and stayed with him and his new family.

For someone doing as poorly in school as Chris was doing, the possibility of low intelligence or a learning disability had to be considered. An evaluation by a school psychologist found Chris to have normal intelligence, but some mild weakness in the perceptual motor areas. As part of a recent remedial tutoring program, his IQ was tested and found to be in the mid-140s. He was not dyslexic, read above class level, and finished serious books in short periods of time and with good comprehension and enjoyment. The intelligence and articulateness he demonstrated in our interviews lent irony to the fact that he was failing the eighth grade.

If Chris was not being held back by a personality or mood disorder, and if he was not seriously cognitively impaired, how do we understand the difficulties he had? I believe Chris became stuck in a strained family dynamic that included the divorce of his parents, the remarriage of his father, and the seemingly chronic depression of his mother. His mother's depression probably inclined him toward depression and passivity, particularly after he was encouraged by his psychiatrist to believe that these traits had been genetically transmitted to him. I suspect that, as Chris became depressed, he felt as if he were fulfilling his destiny. (I'm not exculpating the father here. Let's just say that his possible contributions to Chris's pathology are less evident to me than the mother's.)

I believe that Chris was so confused and overwhelmed by what was going on in his family that he found reasons *not* to use his freedom to stake out a claim for himself in the world. Sartre would say that he allowed his essence to precede his existence. That Chris did not explicitly recognize defaulting in this way does not mean the choice was made with an unconscious component of his psyche. Sartre opposed the notion that human consciousness has an autonomous unconscious component and insisted that mental illness arises from "the free organism, in its total unity." Much of Sartre's writing on psychopathology is implicitly directed against the determinism of Freud, who ceded the ultimate power of thought, emotion, and behavior to a component of the psyche he called the *unconscious*. (In the current dominant paradigm of biological psychiatry, the ultimate power is ceded to neurons and neurotransmitters.)

What we do to slake our desires and fulfill our needs is always chosen, but is not always consciously spelled out or understood as chosen. To Sartre, who equated human existence with freedom, a person can make a free choice without recognizing at the time that a choice is being made. This recognition may or may not come later. As Sartre saw the world, Chris's implicit and paralyzing "I can't do it" was really a choice that meant "I won't do it because it seems too difficult." It is as if Chris were saying, "After all I have been through with my family, how can you expect me to do what most boys my age are doing?" Chris's negation included a refusal to accept much of what the world continued to offer him, even after he found his family situation to be "intolerable." Sartre would say that this self-deceiving, de-differentiating refusal changed the meaning and structure of Chris's existence in a way that made his depression inevitable. (Recall Ed's de-differentiating rejection of his world in chapter 1.)

Ultimately, we all choose what is tolerable or intolerable for us. According to Sartre, the only thing we cannot choose is *not* to choose, even if that choice is made by default. We are, he said, "condemned to freedom." This is our anguish, as well as our glory.

At what age would one be expected to start exercising the freedom that Sartre saw as the essence of our Being? I vividly recall an incident that occurred when I was eight or nine years old. A neighbor was visiting my mother at home. My mother said something to the woman, and I said something that contradicted her. After the woman left, my mother took me aside and insisted, "If I say black is white when someone else is present, black is white." I kept quiet, but thought to myself, "This is not right." I feel certain that my response—which was really a *choice*—was a formative experience for me, creating a psychological template that shaped my subsequent development. At that age, I did not consciously recognize that I was making a choice, or even what it was to make a choice. That did not stop me from choosing what I later came to see as an authentic mode of being rather than an inauthentic mode. Perhaps it was this kind of formative experience that the novelist Graham Greene had in mind when he wrote, "There is always one moment in childhood when the door opens and lets the future in." So far, no comparable "door" seemed to have opened for Chris.

In the three hours I had with Chris, I tried to show him that the person he had become was not the inevitable consequence of influences over which he had no control. I took his eagerness to talk about why his life was going badly, and his willingness to momentarily drop the mask that protected him from a world he chose not to face directly, as signs that he could make less self-deceiving, more authentic choices.

As the thinker who championed freedom and insisted that its misuse could lead to mental illness, Sartre should be allowed the last word here: "Consequently, when in all honesty, I've recognized that man is a being in whom existence precedes essence, that he is a free being who, in various circumstances, can want only his freedom, I have at the same time recognized that I can want only the freedom of others." As clinicians, we should want that kind of empowering freedom for our patients and help them to take hold of it.

Suggested Reading

Chapter 1

Akiskal, H. S. & McKinney, W. T., Jr. (1973), Depressive disorders: Toward a unified hypothesis. *Science,* 18:20–29.

American Psychiatric Association (1993), *Practice Guideline for Major Depressive Disorders in Adults.* Washington, DC: American Psychiatric Association.

American Psychiatric Association (1994), *Diagnostic and Statistical Manual of Mental Disorders, 4th ed.* Washington, DC: American Psychiatric Association, pp. 320–328 [criteria for depression].

Anderson, R. J., Freedland, K. E., Clouse, R. E. & Lustman, P. J. (2001), The prevalence of comorbid depression in adults with diabetes: A meta-analysis. *Diabetes Care,* 24:1069–1078.

Beck, A. T. (1972), *Depression: Cause and Treatment.* Philadelphia: University of Pennsylvania Press.

Beck, A. T. (1987), *Cognitive Treatment of Depression.* New York: Guilford Press.

Burton, R. (1992), *Anatomy of Melancholy.* Kila, MT: Kessinger Publishing.

Damasio, A. R. (1999), *The Feelings of What Happens: Body and Emotion in the Making of Consciousness.* New York: Harcourt Brace Jovanovich.

de Figueiredo, J. M. (1993), Depression and demoralization: Phenomenologic differences and research perspectives. *Compr. Psychiatr.,* 34:308–311.

DePaulo, J. R. & Ablow, K. R. (1989), *How to Cope with Depression: A Complete Guide for You and Your Family.* New York: McGraw-Hill.

Fell, J. P., III (1965), *Emotion in the Thought of Sartre*. New York: Columbia University Press.

Frankl, V. E. (1984), *Man's Search for Meaning: An Introduction to Logotherapy*, 3rd ed. New York: Simon & Schuster.

George, M. S., Ketter, T. A., Parekh, P. I., Horwitz, B., Herscovitch, P. & Post, R. M. (1995), Brain activity during transient sadness and happiness in healthy women. *Amer. J. Psychiatr.,* 152:341–351.

George, M. S., Wasserman, E. M., Kimbrell, T. A., Little, J. T., Williams, W. E., Danielson, A. L., Greenberg, B. D., Hallett, M. & Post, R. M. (1998), Mood improvement following daily left prefrontal repetitive transcranial magnetic stimulation in patients with depression: A placebo-controlled crossover trial. *Amer. J. Psychiatr.,* 154:1752–1756.

Giorgi, A. (1970), *Psychology as a Human Science: A Phenomenologically Based Approach*. New York: Harper & Row.

Giorgi, A., ed. (1985), *Phenomenology and Psychological Research*. Pittsburgh, PA: Duquesne University Press.

Holden, C. (1991), Depression: The news isn't depressing. *Science,* 254: 1450–1452.

Jaspers, K. (1997), *General Psychopathology, Vol. 1,* trans. J. Hoenig & M. W. Hamilton. Baltimore, MD: Johns Hopkins University Press.

Kramer, P. D. (1997), *Listening to Prozac: A Psychiatrist Explores Anti-Depressant Drugs and the Remaking of the Self,* rev. New York: Penguin Books.

Krystal, A. (1986, July 20), Fretting, chafing, sighing, weeping—A toast to the melancholic writer. *New York Times Book Review,* p. 3.

McHugh, P. R. & Slavney, P. R. (1998), *The Perspectives of Psychiatry,* 2nd ed. Baltimore, MD: Johns Hopkins University Press.

Muller, R. J. (1992), When does negative experience lead to depression? In: *Alembics: Baltimore Sketches, Etc.* Baltimore, MD: Icarus Books, pp. 51–52.

Muller, R. J. (2003), Brain changes and placebo [letter]. *Amer. J. Psychiatr.,* 160:389–391.

Muller, R. J. (2003), To understand depression, look to psychobiology, not biopsychiatry. *Psychiatr. Times,* 20(8):41–46.

Sartre, J.-P. (1948), *The Emotions: Outline of a Theory,* trans. B. Frechtman. New York: Wisdom Library.

Sartre, J.-P. (1962), *Existential Psychoanalysis,* trans. H. E. Barnes. Chicago: Henry Regnery.

Styron, W. (1992), *Darkness Visible: A Memoir of Madness*. New York: Vintage Books.

van den Berg, J. H. (1972), *A Different Existence: Principles of Phenomenological Psychopathology.* Pittsburgh, PA: Duquesne University Press.

Whooley, M. A. & Simon, G. E. (2000), Managing depression in medical outpatients. *N. Engl. J. Med.,* 343:1942–1950.

Chapter 2

American Psychiatric Association (1994), *Diagnostic and Statistical Manual of Mental Disorders,* 4th ed. Washington, DC: American Psychiatric Association, pp. 668–669 [criteria for panic disorder].

American Psychiatric Association (1998), *Practice Guideline for the Treatment of Patients with Panic Disorder.* Washington, DC: American Psychiatric Association.

Ballenger, J. C., ed. (1990), *Neurobiology of Panic Disorder.* New York: Wiley.

Barlow, D. H. (1988), *Anxiety and Its Disorders: The Nature and Treatment of Anxiety and Panic.* New York: Guilford Press.

Beck, A. T., Emery, G. & Greenberg, R. L. (1985), *Anxiety Disorders and Phobias: A Cognitive Perspective.* New York: Basic Books.

Corey, M. (1996, October 20), The private pain of a public woman. *Baltimore Sun,* Sec. J, pp. 1, 4.

Gorman, J. M., Kent, J. M., Sullivan, G. M. & Coplan, J. D. (2000), Neuroanatomical hypothesis of panic disorder, revised. *Amer. J. Psychiatr.,* 157: 493–505.

Hall, S. S. (1999, February 28), Fear itself: What we now know about how it works, how it can be treated and what it tells us about our unconscious. *New York Times Magazine,* pp. 42–47, 69–70, 72, 88–89, 91.

Klerman, G. L. (1991, February), Panic disorder: Strategies for long-term treatment. *J. Clin. Psychiatr.,* 52:2(Suppl.).

Klerman, G. L., Hirschfeld, R. M. A., Weissman, M. M., Pelicier, Y., Ballenger, J. C., Costa e Silva, J. A., Judd, L. L. & Keller, M. B., eds. (1993), *Panic Anxiety and Its Treatments: Report of the World Psychiatric Association Presidential Educational Program Task Force.* Washington, DC: American Psychiatric Press.

Levine, D. (1999, September), Prone to panic. *Johns Hopkins Magazine,* pp. 13–17.

Noyes, R., Jr. & Hoehn-Saric, R. (1998), *The Anxiety Disorders.* New York: Cambridge University Press.

Persons, J. B. (1992), A case formulation approach to cognitive-behavior therapy: Application to panic disorder. *Psychiatr. Ann.,* 22:470–473.

Rosenbaum, J. F. & Pollack, M. H., eds. (1998), *Panic Disorder and Its Treatment.* New York: Marcel Dekker.

Shear, M. K., Cooper, A. M., Klerman, G. L., Busch, F. N. & Shapiro, T. (1993), A psychodynamic model of panic disorder. *Amer. J. Psychiatr.,* 150:859–865.

Chapter 3

American Psychiatric Association (1994), *Diagnostic and Statistical Manual of Mental Disorders,* 4th ed. Washington, DC: American Psychiatric Association, pp. 650–654 [criteria for borderline personality disorder].

Brockman, R. (1998), *A Map of the Mind: Toward a Science of Psychotherapy.* Madison, CT: Psychosocial Press.

Clarkin, J. F., Yeomans, F. E. & Kernberg, O. F. (1999), *Psychotherapy for Borderline Personality.* New York: Wiley.

Fitzgerald, F. S. (1993), *The Crack-Up,* ed. E. Wilson. New York: New Directions.

Grotstein, J. S. (1997), *Splitting and Projective Identification.* Northvale, NJ: Aronson.

Gunderson, J. G. (2001), *Borderline Personality Disorder: A Clinical Guide.* Washington, DC: American Psychiatric Press.

Kernberg, O. F. (1975), *Borderline Conditions and Pathological Narcissism.* New York: Aronson.

Lewin, R. A. & Schulz, C. (1992), *Losing and Fusing: Borderline Transitional Objects and Self Relations.* Northvale, NJ: Aronson.

Linehan, M. M. (1993), *Cognitive-Behavioral Treatment of Borderline Personality Disorder.* New York: Guilford Press.

Masterson, J. F. (1976), *Psychotherapy of the Borderline Adult: A Developmental Approach.* New York: Brunner/Mazel.

Muller, R. J. (1991), Distinguishing borderline patients with splitting [letter]. *Amer. J. Psychiatr.,* 148:1404–1405.

Muller, R. J. (1992), Depression in borderline patients who split [letter]. *Amer. J. Psychiatr.,* 149:580–58.

Muller, R. J. (1992), Is there a neural basis for borderline splitting? *Compr. Psychiatr.,* 33:92–104.

Muller, R. J. (1994), *Anatomy of a Splitting Borderline: Description and Analysis of a Case History.* Westport, CT: Praeger.

Muller, R. J. (1998), A borderline patient splits in—and from—the ER. *Psychiatr. Times,* 15(9):18–19.

Stone, M. H. (1990), *The Fate of Borderline Patients: Successful Outcome and Psychiatric Practice.* New York: Guilford Press.

Summers, F. (1994), *Object Relations Theories and Psychopathology: A Comprehensive Text.* Hillsdale, NJ: The Analytic Press.

Wilkinson-Ryan, T. & Westen, D. (2000), Identity disturbance in borderline personality disorder: An empirical investigation. *Amer. J. Psychiatr.,* 157: 528–541.

Chapter 4

Acocella, J. (1999), *Creating Hysteria: Women and MPD.* San Francisco: Jossey-Bass.

American Psychiatric Association (1994), *Diagnostic and Statistical Manual of Mental Disorders,* 4th ed. Washington, DC: American Psychiatric Association, pp. 484–488 [criteria for multiple personality disorder/dissociative identity disorder].

Khantzian, E. J. (1999), *Treating Addiction as a Human Process.* Northvale, NJ: Aronson.

McHugh, P. R. (1992), Psychiatric misadventures. *Amer. Schol.,* 61:497–510.

McHugh, P. R. (1995), Witches, multiple personalities and other psychiatric artifacts. *Nat. Med.,* 1:110–114.

McHugh, P. R. (1999, December), How psychiatry lost its way. *Commentary,* pp. 32–38.

McHugh, P. R. & Putnam, F. W. (1995), Resolved: Multiple personality disorder is an individually and socially created artifact. *J. Amer. Acad. Child Adolesc. Psychiatr.,* 34:957–962; discussion, 962–963.

Merskey, H. (1992), The manufacture of personalities: The production of multiple personality disorder. *Brit. J. Psychiatr.,* 160:327–340 [see comments].

Muller, R. J. (1998), A patient with dissociative identity disorder "switches" in the emergency room. *Psychiatr. Times,* 15(11):7–9.

Putnam, F. W. (1989), *Diagnosis and Treatment of Multiple Personality Disorder.* New York: Guilford Press.

Ross, C. A. (1989), *Multiple Personality Disorder: Diagnosis, Clinical Features, and Treatment.* New York: Wiley.

Thigpen, C. H. & Cleckley, H. M. (1957), *The Three Faces of Eve.* New York: McGraw-Hill.

Chapters 5 and 6

American Psychiatric Association (1994), *Diagnostic and Statistical Manual of Mental Disorders,* 4th ed. Washington, DC: American Psychiatric Association, pp. 175–272 [criteria for substance-related disorders].

American Psychiatric Association (1995), *Practice Guideline for the Treatment of Patients with Substance Use Disorders: Alcohol, Cocaine, Opioids.* Washington, DC: American Psychiatric Association.

Brick, J. & Erickson, C. (1998), *Drugs, the Brain, and Behavior: The Pharmacology of Abuse and Dependence.* Binghamton, NY: Haworth Medical Press.

Dajer, T. (1998, October), Snowed. *Discovery,* pp. 40–44.

Forrest, G. G. (1994), *Alcoholism, Narcissism and Psychopathology.* Northvale, NJ: Aronson.

Galanter, M. & Klebert, H. D., eds. (1999), *The American Psychiatric Press Textbook of Substance Abuse Treatment,* 2nd ed. Washington, DC: American Psychiatric Association.

Gold, M. S. (1989), *Marijuana.* New York: Plenum Press.

Gold, M. S. & Galanter, M., eds. (1987), *Cocaine: Pharmacology, Addiction and Therapy.* Binghamton, NY: Haworth Press.

Halpern, J. H. (2002), Addiction is a disease. *Psychiatr. Times,* 19(10):55–60.

Hart, R. H. (1980), *Bitter Grass: The Cruel Truth About Marijuana.* Sun City West, AZ: Menta.

Lancaster, J. (2003, January 6), High style: Writing under the influence. *New Yorker,* pp. 80–84.

Leshner, A. I. (1997), Drug abuse and addiction treatment: The next generation. *Arch. Gen. Psychiatr.,* 54:691–694.

Levinthal, C. F. (1988), *Messengers of Paradise: Opiates and the Brain.* New York: Anchor Press/Doubleday.

Lieber, C. S. (1995), Medical disorders of alcoholism. *N. Engl. J. Med.,* 333: 1058–1065.

Mendelson, J. H. & Mello, N. K. (1996), Management of cocaine abuse and dependence. *N. Engl. J. Med.,* 334:965–972.

Muller, R. J. (1992), An alcoholic who drinks is ill *and* willfully misbehaving. In: *Alembics: Baltimore Sketches, Etc.* Baltimore, MD: Icarus Books, pp. 45–46.

O'Brien, C. P. & McLellan, A. T. (1996), Myths about the treatment of addiction. *Lancet,* 347:237–240.

Perrine, D. M. (1996), *The Chemistry of Mind-Altering Drugs: History, Pharmacology, and Cultural Context.* Washington, DC: American Chemical Society (New York: Oxford University Press, distributor).

Randall, T. (1992), Cocaine, alcohol mix in body to form even longer lasting, more lethal drug. *J. Amer. Med. Assn.,* 267:1043–1044.

Schaler, J. A. (2002), Addiction is a choice. *Psychiatr. Times,* 19(10):54–62.

Shenk, J. W. (1999, May), America's altered states: When does legal relief of pain become illegal pursuit of pleasure? *Harper's,* pp. 38–52.

Stone, R. (1986, December), A higher horror of the whiteness: Cocaine's coloring of the American psyche. *Harper's,* pp. 49–54.

Swift, R. M. (1999), Drug therapy for alcohol dependence. *N. Engl. J. Med.,* 340: 1482–1490.

Vaillant, G. (1993), Is alcoholism more often the cause or the result of depression? *Harvard Rev. Psychiatr.,* 1:94–99.

Vaillant, G. (1995), The Natural History of Alcoholism Revisited. Cambridge, MA: Harvard University Press.

Zackon, F. & McAulyfe, W. E. (1986), *Heroin: The Street Narcotic.* Broomall, PA: Chelsea House.

Chapters 7 and 8

American Psychiatric Association (1994), *Diagnostic and Statistical Manual of Mental Disorders,* 4th ed. Washington, DC: American Psychiatric Association, pp. 350–358 [criteria for bipolar I disorder].

American Psychiatric Association (1995), *Practice Guideline for the Treatment of Patients with Bipolar Disorder.* Washington, DC: American Psychiatric Association.

Andreasen, N. C. & Glick, I. D. (1988), Bipolar affective disorder and creativity: Implications and clinical management. *Compr. Psychiatr.,* 29:207–217.

Fieve, R. R. (1989), *Moodswing,* rev. New York: Bantam Books.

Goldberg, J. F. & Harrow, M., eds. (1999), *Bipolar Disorders: Clinical Course and Outcome.* Washington, DC: American Psychiatric Press.

Goodnick, P. J., ed. (1998), *Mania: Clinical and Research Perspectives.* Washington, DC: American Psychiatric Press.

Goodwin, F. K. & Jamison, K. R. (1990), *Manic-Depressive Illness.* New York: Oxford University Press.

Grisaru, N., Chudakov, B., Yaroslavsky, Y. & Belmaker, R. H. (1998), Transcranial magnetic stimulation in mania: A controlled study. *Amer. J. Psychiatr.,* 155:1608–1610.

Hershman, D. J. & Lieb, J. (1988), *The Key to Genius: Manic Depression and the Creative Life.* New York: Prometheus Books.

Jamison, K. R. (1994), *Touched with Fire: Manic-Depressive Illness and the Artistic Temperament.* New York: Free Press Paperbacks.

Jamison, K. R. (1995), *An Unquiet Mind: A Memoir of Moods and Madness.* New York: Knopf.

Kane, J. M. (1988), The role of neuroleptics in manic-depressive illness. *J. Clin. Psychiatr.,* 49(Suppl.):12–14.

Keck, P. E., Jr., McElroy, S. L., Tugrul, K. C. & Bennett, J. A. (1993), Valproate oral loading in the treatment of acute mania. *J. Clin. Psychiatr.,* 54:305–308.

Keck, P. E., Jr., McElroy, S. L. & Strakowski, S. M. (1998), Anticonvulsants and antipsychotics in the treatment of bipolar disorder. *J. Clin. Psychiatr.,* 49(Suppl. 6):74–81.

Middlebrook, D. W. (1991), *Anne Sexton: A Biography.* Boston: Houghton Mifflin.

Mondimore, F. M. (1999), *Bipolar Disorder: A Guide for Patients and Families.* Baltimore, MD: Johns Hopkins University Press.

Post, R. M., Uhde, T. W., Ballenger, J. C. & Squillace, K. M. (1983), Prophylactic efficacy of carbamazepine in manic-depressive illness. *Amer. J. Psychiatr.,* 140:1602–1604.

Steel, D. (1998), *His Bright Light: The Story of Nick Traina.* New York: Delacorte Press.

Wigoder, D. (1987), *Images of Destruction.* New York: Routledge & Kegan Paul.

Winokur, G. (1970), The natural history of the affective disorders (manias and depressions). *Semin. Psychiatr.,* 2:451–463.

Zarate, C. A., Jr., Tohen, M. & Baldessarini, R. J. (1995), Clozapine in severe mood disorders. *J. Clin. Psychiatr.,* 56:411–417.

Chapter 9

American Psychiatric Association (1994), *Diagnostic and Statistical Manual of Mental Disorders,* 4th ed. Washington, DC: American Psychiatric Association, pp. 274–290 [criteria for schizophrenia].

American Psychiatric Association (1997), *Practice Guideline for the Treatment of Patients with Schizophrenia.* Washington, DC: American Psychiatric Association.

Andreasen, N. C. (1999), Understanding the causes of schizophrenia. *N. Engl. J. Med.,* 340:645–647.

Arieti, S. (1974), *Interpretation of Schizophrenia,* 2nd ed. New York: Basic Books.

Belkin, L. (1999, March 14), What the Jumans didn't know about Michael: The adoption agency never mentioned his genetic legacy—Schizophrenia. The consequences were devastating. *New York Times Magazine*, pp. 42, 44–49.

Carpenter, W. T. & Buchanan, R. W. (1994), Schizophrenia. *N. Engl. J. Med.*, 330:681–690.

Foucault, M., ed. (1975), *I, Pierre Rivière, Having Slaughtered My Mother, My Sister, and My Brother...: A Case of Parricide in the 19th Century*, trans. F. Jellinek. Lincoln: University of Nebraska Press.

Kasanin, J. S. (1964), *Language and Thought in Schizophrenia*. New York: Norton.

Muller, R. J. (2000), A floridly decompensated schizophrenic patient in the ER. *Psychiatr. Times*, 17(12):49.

Tamminga, C. A., ed. (1999), *Schizophrenia in a Molecular Age*. Washington, DC: American Psychiatric Press.

Torrey, E. F. (1995), *Surviving Schizophrenia: A Manual for Families, Consumers, and Providers*, 3rd ed. New York: HarperCollins.

Vonnegut, M. (1988), *The Eden Express*. New York: Dell.

Whitehouse, P. J., Maurer, K. & Ballenger, J. F., eds. (2000), *Concepts of Alzheimer Disease: Biological, Clinical, and Cultural Perspectives*. Baltimore, MD: Johns Hopkins University Press.

Winchester, S. (1998), *The Professor and the Madman: A Tale of Murder, Insanity, and the Making of the* Oxford English Dictionary. New York: HarperCollins.

Winerip, M. (1999, May 23), Bedlam on the streets: Increasingly, the mentally ill have nowhere to go. That's their problem—and ours. *New York Times Magazine*, pp. 42, 44–49, 56, 65–66, 70.

Wyden, P. (1998), *Conquering Schizophrenia: A Father, His Son, and a Medical Breakthrough*. New York: Knopf.

Chapter 10

American Psychiatric Association (1994), *Diagnostic and Statistical Manual of Mental Disorders*, 4th ed. Washington, DC: American Psychiatric Association, pp. 139–143 [criteria for dementia of the Alzheimer's type].

American Psychiatric Association (1997), *Practice Guideline for the Treatment of Patients with Alzheimer's Disease and Other Dementias of Late Life*. Washington, DC: American Psychiatric Association.

Bailey, J. (1998), *Elegy for Iris*. New York: St. Martin's Press.

Coffey, C. E. & Cummings, J. L., eds. (1994), *The American Psychiatric Press Textbook of Geriatric Neuropsychiatry*. Washington, DC: American Psychiatric Association.

Ernaus, A. (1999), *"I Remain in Darkness,"* trans. T. Leslie. New York: Seven Stories Press.

Mace, N. L. & Rabins, P. V. (1991), *The Thirty-Six Hour Day: A Family Guide to Caring for Persons with Alzheimer's Disease, Related Dementing Illnesses and Memory Loss in Later Life*, 2nd ed. Baltimore, MD: Johns Hopkins University Press.

Martin, J. B. (1999), Molecular basis of the neurodegenerative disorders. *N. Engl. J. Med.,* 340:1970–1980.

Mayeux, R. & Sano, M. (1999), Treatment of Alzheimer's disease. *N. Engl. J. Med.,* 341:1670–1679.

Young, E. P. (1999), *Between Two Worlds: Special Moments of Alzheimer's and Dementia*. Amherst, NY: Prometheus Books.

Chapter 11

American Psychiatric Association (1994), *Diagnostic and Statistical Manual of Mental Disorders*, 4th ed. Washington, DC: American Psychiatric Association, pp. 668–669 [criteria for panic disorder]; pp. 665–669 [criteria for dependent personality disorder].

Bornstein, R. F. (1992), The dependent personality: Developmental, social, and clinical perspectives. *Psychol. Bull.,* 112:3–23.

Bornstein, R. F. (1995), Active dependency. *J. Nerv. Ment. Dis.,* 183:64–77.

Bornstein, R. F. (1998), Depathologizing dependency. *J. Nerv. Ment. Dis.,* 186: 67–73.

Gitlin, M. J. (1993), Pharmacotherapy of personality disorders: Conceptual framework and clinical strategies. *J. Clin. Psychopharmacol.,* 13:343–353.

Millon, T. (1987), *Millon Clinical Multiaxial Inventory–II*. Minneapolis, MN: National Computer Systems.

Muller, R. J. (1999), A patient with panic disorder abetted by a dependent personality. *Psychiatr. Times,* 16(11):12–13.

Chapter 12

American Psychiatric Association (1994), *Diagnostic and Statistical Manual of Mental Disorders*, 4th ed. Washington, DC: American Psychiatric Association, pp. 328–332 [criteria for mania]; pp. 655–658 [criteria for histrionic personality disorder].

Cloninger, C. R., ed. (1999), *Personality and Psychopathology*. Washington, DC: American Psychiatric Press.

Liebowitz, M. R. & Klein, D. F. (1981), Interrelationship of hysteroid dysphoria and borderline personality disorder. *Psychiatr. Clin. North Amer.*, 4:67–87. Philadelphia, PA.

Millon, T. (1996), *Disorders of Personality: DSM-IV and Beyond*, 2nd ed. New York: Wiley.

Muller, R. J. (1999), An ER patient with a personality disorder misdiagnosed as schizophrenia. *Psychiatr. Times*, 16(1):37–38; comments, 16(6):73–74.

Ofshe, R. & Watters, E. (1994), *Making Monsters: False Memories, Psychotherapy, and Sexual Hysteria*. New York: Scribner's.

Schacter, D. L. (1996), *Searching for Memory: The Brain, the Mind, and the Past*. New York: Basic Books.

Slavney, P. R. (1990), *Perspectives on "Hysteria."* Baltimore, MD: Johns Hopkins University Press.

Spence, D. P. (1982), *Narrative Truth and Historical Truth: Meaning and Interpretation in Psychoanalysis*. New York: Norton.

Stone, M. H. (1993), *Abnormalities of Personality: Within and Beyond the Realm of Treatment*. New York: Norton.

Westen, D. & Shedler, J. (1999), Revising and assessing Axis II, Part II: Toward an empirically based and clinically useful classification of personality disorders. *Amer. J. Psychiatr.*, 156:273–285.

Chapter 13

American Psychiatric Association (1994), *Diagnostic and Statistical Manual of Mental Disorders*, 4th ed. Washington, DC: American Psychiatric Association, p. 683.

Andrews, T. C., Cull, D. L., Pelton, J. J., Massey, S. O., Jr. & Bostwick, J. M. (1997), Self-mutilation and malingering among Cuban migrants detained at Guantanamo Bay. *N. Engl. J. Med.*, 336:1251.

Drewry, W. F. (1996), Feigned insanity: Report of three cases. *J. Amer. Med. Assn.*, 276:1356. See also: Martensen, R. L. (1996), The detection of feigned insanity. *J. Amer. Med. Assn.*, 276:1357.

Eisendrath, S. J. (1996, Fall), When Munchausen becomes malingering: Factitious disorders that penetrate the legal system. *Bull. Amer. Acad. Psychiatr. Law*, 24:471–481.

McKane, J. P. & Anderson, J. (1994), Munchausen's syndrome: Rule breakers and risk takers. *Brit. J. Hosp. Med.*, 58:150–153.

Muller, R. J. (1998), Malingerers and manipulators in the ER. *Psychiatr. Times,*
    15(3):23–25; comments, 15(6):9–10.
Schreier, H. A. & Libow, J. A. (1993), *Hurting for Love: Munchausen by Proxy Syn-*
    drome. New York: Guilford Press.

Chapters 14 and 15

Muller, R. J. (2003), "Dumps" and "stumbles" in the ER. *Psychiatr. Times,*
    20(5):70–72.

Chapter 17

American Psychiatric Association (1994), *Diagnostic and Statistical Manual of Men-*
    tal Disorders, 4th ed. Washington, DC: American Psychiatric Association,
    pp. 274–290 [criteria for schizophrenia].
Bailey, D. N., Coffee, J. J., Anderson, B. & Manoguerra, A. S. (1992), Interac-
    tion of tricyclic antidepressants with cholestyramine in vitro. *Ther. Drug*
    Monit., 14:339–342.
Brown, T. M. & Stoudemire, A. (1998), *Psychiatric Side Effects of Prescription and*
    Over-the-Counter Medications: Recognition and Management. Washington, DC:
    American Psychiatric Press.
Muller, R. J. (1997, March), Why is this schizophrenic patient hearing voices?
    Psychiatr. Times, p. 37.
Phillips, W. A., Ratchford, J. M. & Schultz, J. R. (1976), Effects of
    colestipol hydrochloride on drug absorption in the rat. *J. Pharm. Sci.,*
    65:1285–1291.

Chapter 18

Ferrando, S. J. & Eisendrath, S. J. (1991), Adverse neuropsychiatric effects of
    dopamine antagonist medications: Misdiagnosis in the medical setting.
    Psychosomatics, 32:426–432.
Perry, P. J., Alexander, B. & Liskow, B. I. (1997), *Psychotropic Drug Handbook,* 7th
    ed. Washington, DC: American Psychiatric Association.
Schatzberg, A. F., Cole, J. O. & DeBattista, C. (1997), *Manual of Clinical*
    Psychopharmacology, 3rd ed. Washington, DC: American Psychiatric
    Association.

Chapter 19

Christensen, R. C. (1995), Misdiagnosis of anticholinergic delirium as schizophrenic psychosis [letter]. *Amer. J. Emerg. Med.,* 13(1):117–118.

Duvoisin, R. & Katz, R. (1968), Reversal of central anticholinergic syndrome in man by physostigmine. *J. Amer. Med. Assn.,* 206:1963–1965.

Frezza, M., di Padova, C., Pozzato, G., Terpin, M., Baraona, E. & Lieber, C. S. (1990), High blood alcohol levels in women: The role of decreased gastric alcohol dehydrogenase activity and first-pass metabolism. *N. Engl. J. Med.,* 322:95–99.

Goldfrank, L. R., ed. (1998), *Goldfrank's Toxicologic Emergencies,* 6th ed. Stamford, CT: Appleton & Lange.

Muller, R. J. (1999), A serious overdose, but of what? *Psychiatr. Times,* 16(3):54.

National Institute on Alcohol Abuse and Alcoholism (1994, January), *Alcohol Alert,* No. 23 PH 347 [information on alcohol and minorities].

Zareba, W., Moss, A. J., Rosero, S. Z., Hajj-Ali, R., Konecki, J. & Andrews, M. (1997), Electrocardiographic findings in patients with diphenhydramine overdose. *Amer. J. Cardiol.,* 80:1168–1173.

Chapter 20

Alexander, M. P. (1995), Mild traumatic brain injury: Pathophysiology, natural history, and clinical management. *Neurology,* 45:1253–1260.

Andreasen, N. C. (1999), Understanding the causes of schizophrenia. *N. Engl. J. Med.,* 340:645–647.

Deb, S., Lyons, I., Koutzoukis, C., Ali, I. & McCarthy, G. (1999), Rate of psychiatric illness 1 year after traumatic brain injury. *Amer. J. Psychiatr.,* 156: 374–378.

Frieboes, R. M., Müller, U. & vonCramon, D. Y. (1994), Literaturübersicht und fallbericht. *Nervenarzt,* 65:707–711.

Fujii, D. (2002), Neuropsychiatry of psychosis secondary to traumatic brain injury. *Psychiatr. Times,* 19(8):33–35.

Fujii, D. E. & Ahmed, I. (1996), Psychosis secondary to traumatic brain injury. *Neuropsychiatr. Neuropsychol. Behav. Neurol.,* 9:133–138.

Fujii, D. E. & Ahmed, I. (2002), Psychotic disorder following traumatic brain injury: A conceptual framework. *Cogn. Neuropsychiatr.,* 7(1):41–62.

Gualtieri, T. C. (2002), *Brain Injury and Mental Retardation.* Philadelphia, PA: Lippincott, Williams & Wilkins.

McAllister, T. W. (1992), Neuropsychiatric sequelae of head injuries. *Psychiatr. Clin. North Amer.,* 15:395–413.

Muller, R. J. (2001), A patient who developed psychotic symptoms after a minor traumatic brain injury. *Psychiatr. Times,* 18(6):58–62.

Nasrallah, H. A., Fowler, R. C. & Judd, L. L. (1981), Schizophrenia-like illness following head injury. *Psychosomatics,* 22:359–361.

Sandel, M. E., Olive, D. A. & Rader, M. A. (1993), Chlorpromazine-induced psychosis after brain injury. *Brain Inj.,* 7:77–83.

van Reekum, R., Bolago, I., Finlayson, M. A. J., Garner, S. & Links, P. S. (1996), Psychiatric disorders after traumatic brain injury. *Brain Inj.,* 10:319–327.

Victoroff, J. (1999, November), Minor head trauma, major trouble. *Psychiatr. Times,* pp. 45–46.

Chapter 21

Adams, R. D., Victor, M. & Ropper, A. H., eds. (1997), *Principles of Neurology,* 6th ed. New York: McGraw-Hill, p. 550.

Buff, D. D. & Markowitz, S. (2003), Hyponatremia in the psychiatric patient: A review of diagnostic and management strategies. *Psychiatr. Ann.,* 33:318–325.

Cronin, R. E. (1987), Psychogenic polydipsia with hyponatremia: Report of eleven cases. *Amer. J. Kidney Dis.,* 9:410–416.

Emsley, R. A., Spangenberg, J. J., Roberts, M. C., Taljaard, F. J. & Chalton, D. O. (1993), Disordered water homeostasis and cognitive impairment in schizophrenia. *Biol. Psychiatr.,* 34:630–633.

Leadbetter, R. A., Shutty, M. S., Elkashef, A. M., Kirch, D. G., Spraggins, T., Cail, W. S., Wu, H., Bilder, R. M., Lieberman, J. A. & Wyatt, R. J. (1999), MRI changes during water loading in patients with polydipsia and intermittent hyponatremia. *Amer. J. Psychiatr.,* 156:958–960.

Muller, R. J. (1998), Falling through the cracks: Intractable hiccups, severe psychogenic polydipsia and hyponatremia. *Psychiatr. Times,* 15(6):20–22.

Muller, R. J. & Lann, H. D. (1991), Thiazide diuretics and polydipsia in schizophrenic patients [letter]. *Amer. J. Psychiatr.,* 148:390.

Ramirez, F. C. & Graham, D. Y. (1992), Treatment of intractable hiccup with baclofen: Results of a double-blind randomized, controlled, cross-over study. *Amer. J. Gastroenterol.,* 87:1789–1791.

Ramirez, F. C. & Graham, D. Y. (1993), Hiccups, compulsive water drinking, and hyponatremia [letter]. *Ann. Intern. Med.,* 118:649.

Riggs, A. T., Dysken, M. W., Kim, S. W. & Opsahl, J. A. (1991), A review of disorders of water homeostasis in psychiatric patients. *Psychosomatics,* 32: 133–148.

Schnur, D. B. & Kirch, D. G., eds. (1996), *Water Balance in Schizophrenia.* Washington, DC: American Psychiatric Press.

Chapter 22

American Psychiatric Association (1994), *Diagnostic and Statistical Manual of Mental Disorders,* 4th ed. Washington, DC: American Psychiatric Association, pp. 123–133 [criteria for delirium].

Asher, R. (1949), Myxoedematous madness. *Brit. Med. J.,* 2:555–562.

Barton, C. H., Sterling, M. L. & Vaziri, N. D. (1980), Rhabdomyolysis and acute renal failure associated with phencyclidine intoxication. *Arch. Intern. Med.,* 140:568–569.

Bayliss, R. I. S. (1998), Myxoedematous madness and the Citadel. *J. Royal Soc. Med.,* 91:149–151.

Case Records of the Massachusetts General Hospital (2001), [Case 12-2001]. *N. Engl. J. Med.,* 344:1232–1239.

Darko, D. F. Krull, A., Dickinson, M., Gillin, J. C. & Risch, S. C. (1988), The diagnostic dilemma of myxedema and madness, Axis I and Axis II: A longitudinal case report. *Internat. J. Psychiatr. Med.,* 18:263–270.

Katz, J., Prescott, K. & Woolf, A. D. (1996), Strychnine poisoning from a Cambodian traditional remedy. *Amer. J. Emerg. Med.,* 14:475–477.

Lewis, L. M., Miller, D. K., Morley, J. E., Nork, M. J. & Lasater, L. C. (1995), Unrecognized delirium in ED geriatric patients. *Amer. J. Emerg. Med.,* 13: 142–145.

Libow, L. S. & Durell, J. (1965), Clinical studies on the relationship between psychosis and the regulation of thyroid gland activity. *Psychosom. Med.,* 28: 377–382.

Lipowski, Z. J. (1990), *Delirium: Acute Confusional States.* New York: Oxford University Press.

Liptzin, B. & Levkoff, S. E. (1992), An empirical study of delirium subtypes. *Brit. J. Psychiatr.,* 161:843–845.

Manos, P. J. & Wu, R. (1994), The ten-point clock test: A quick screen and grading method for cognitive impairment in medical and surgical patients. *Internat. J. Psychiatr. Med.,* 24:229–244.

McHugh, P. R. (1992), Psychiatric misadventures. *Amer. Schol.,* 61:497–510.

Muller, R. J. (1998), Falling through the cracks: Intractable hiccups, severe psychogenic polydipsia and hyponatremia. *Psychiatr. Times,* 15(6):20–22.

Muller, R. J. (1999), A serious overdose, but of what? *Psychiatr. Times,* 16(3):54.

Muller, R. J. (2002), Delirium missed as the cause of psychotic symptoms in the ER. *Psychiatr. Times,* 19(12):68–74.

Ryan, C. J. & Anderson, J. (2001), Case 12-2001: Strychnine poisoning [letter]. *N. Engl. J. Med.,* 345:1577.

Slavney, P. R. (1998), *Psychiatric Dimensions of Medical Practice: What Primary-Care Physicians Should Know About Delirium, Demoralization, Suicidal Thinking, and Competence to Refuse Medical Attention.* Baltimore, MD: Johns Hopkins University Press, pp. 9–62.

Smith, B. A. (1990), Strychnine poisoning [published correction appears in *J. Emerg. Med.,* 1991;9:555]. *J. Emerg. Med.,* 8:321–325.

Chapter 23

Charon, R. (1999, March 10), Narrative competence in medicine: Working in the dark, doing what we can, giving what we have. Paper presented at: Johns Hopkins Medical Institutions, Baltimore, MD.

Damasio, A. R. (1999), *The Feeling of What Happens: Body and Emotion in the Making of Consciousness.* New York: Harcourt Brace Jovanovich.

Danto, A. C. (1985), *Narratives and Knowledge.* New York: Columbia University Press.

Gustafson, J. P. (1991, November), New narrative directions: So-called personality disorders and brief psychotherapy. *Psychiatr. Times,* pp. 44, 46.

Gustafson, J. P. (1992), *Self-Delight in a Harsh World.* New York: Norton.

Hawkins, A. H. (1993), *Reconstructing Illness: Studies in Pathography.* West Lafayette, IN: Purdue University Press.

James, H. (1984), The middle years. In: *Tales of Henry James,* ed. C. Wegelin. New York: Norton, pp. 260–276.

Muller, R. J. (2000), The narrative in psychiatric diagnosis. *Psychiatr. Times,* 17(2):14–15.

Polkinghorne, D. E. (1988), *Narrative Knowing and the Human Sciences.* Albany: State University of New York Press.

Rosenhan, D. L. (1973), On being sane in insane places. *Science,* 179:250–258.

Spence, D. P. (1982), *Narrative Truth and Historical Truth: Meaning and Interpretation in Psychoanalysis.* New York: Norton.

Van den Broek, P. & Thurlow, R. (1991), The role and structure of personal narratives. *J. Cogn. Psychother.,* 5:257–274.

White, M. & Epston, D. (1990), *Narrative Means to Therapeutic Ends.* New York: Norton.

Chapter 24

Cohen, I. H. (1987), Masked depression revisited. *Maryland Med. J.,* 36:571.

Egan, J. (1997, July 27), The thin red line. *New York Times Magazine,* pp. 21–25, 34, 40, 43, 44, 48.

Fisch, R. Z. & Nesher, G. (1986), Masked depression: Help for the hidden misery. *Postgrad. Med.,* 80:165–169.

Kooiman, C. G. (1998), The status of alexithymia as a risk factor in medically unexplained physical symptoms. *Compr. Psychiatr.,* 39:152–159.

Leibenluft, E., Gardner, D. L. & Cowdry, R. W. (1987), The inner experience of the borderline self-mutilator. *J. Pers. Disord.,* 1:317–324.

Lesser, I. M. (1981), A review of the alexithymia concept. *Psychosom. Med.,* 43: 531–543.

Lesser, I. M. (1984), Current concepts in psychiatry: Alexithymia. *N. Engl. J. Med.,* 312:690–692.

Levenkron, S. (1998), *Cutting: Understanding and Overcoming Self-Mutilation.* New York: Norton.

Lumley, M. A., Stettner, L. & Wehmer, F. (1996), How are alexithymia and physical illness linked? A review and critique of pathways. *J. Psychosom. Res.,* 41:505–518.

Muller, R. J. (2000), When a patient has no story to tell: Alexithymia. *Psychiatr. Times,* 17(7):71–72.

Nemiah, J. C. (1975), Denial revisited: Reflections on psychosomatic theory. *Psychother. Psychosom.,* 26:140–147.

Nemiah, J. C. (1977), Alexithymia: Theoretical considerations. *Psychother. Psychosom.,* 28:199–206.

Sifneos, P. E. (1972), *Short-Term Psychotherapy and Emotional Crisis.* Cambridge, MA: Harvard University Press.

Sifneos, P. E. (1996), Alexithymia: Past and present. *Amer. J. Psychiatr.,* 153(7 Suppl.):137–142.

Simon, G. E., VonKorff, M., Piccinelli, M., Fullerton, C. & Ormel, J. (1999), An international study of the relation between somatic symptoms and depression. *N. Engl. J. Med.,* 341:1329–1335.

Stoudemire, A. (1991), Somatothymia. *Psychosomatics,* 32:365–381.

Taylor, G. J. (1984), Alexithymia: Concept, measurement, and indications for treatment. *Amer. J. Psychiatr.,* 141:725–732.

Taylor, G. J., Bagby, R. M. & Parker, J. D. (1991), The alexithymia construct: A potential paradigm for psychosomatic medicine. *Psychosomatics,* 32: 153–164.

Zeitlin, S. B., McNally, R. J. & Cassiday, K. L. (1993), Alexithymia in victims of sexual assault: An effect of repeated traumatization? *Amer. J. Psychiatr.,* 150: 661–663.

Chapter 25

Lahr, J. (2001, October 15), The alchemist. *New Yorker,* 77(31):88–96.

Muller, R. J. (1998), Malingerers and manipulators in the ER. *Psychiatr. Times,* 15(3):23–25; comments, 15(6):9–10.

Muller, R. J. (2002), Renegotiating the "contract for safety" in the ER. *Psychiatr. Times,* 19(5):56–58; comments, 19(8):53.

Chapter 26

Desan, W. (1954), *The Tragic Finale: An Essay on the Philosophy of Jean-Paul Sartre.* Cambridge, MA: Harvard University Press.

Fell, J. P. (1965), *Emotion in the Thought of Sartre.* New York: Columbia University Press.

Fingarette, H. (1969), *Self-Deception.* London: Routledge & Kegan Paul.

Laing, R. D. & Cooper, D. G. (1964), *Reason and Violence: A Decade of Sartre's Philosophy (1950–1960).* London: Tavistock, p. 7.

Muller, R. J. (1987), *The Marginal Self: An Existential Inquiry into Narcissism.* Atlantic Highlands, NJ: Humanities Press International.

Muller, R. J. (2002), Between the ivory tower and the trenches: Jean-Paul Sartre in the ER. *Psychiatr. Times,* 19(6):26–28; comments, 2003;20(1):10–11.

Sartre, J.-P. (1956), *Being and Nothingness: An Essay on Phenomenological Ontology,* trans. H. Barnes. New York: Philosophical Library.